Experiencing
God in Goodbye

*Saying Goodbye is Both Painful and
Sweet If You Look to God for the Strength
and Comfort He Gives So Tenderly*

Tonette Blasius

ISBN 978-1-68570-045-4 (paperback)
ISBN 978-1-68570-046-1 (digital)

Christian Faith Publishing
832 Park Avenue
Meadville, PA 16335
www.christianfaithpublishing.com

Printed in the United States of America

In memory of my mother, Betty Doris (Easter) Edde February 10, 1942–June 06, 2021.

Contents

Introduction

I recently had to say goodbye to my mother. What I must tell you is that my relationship with my mother was strained at times, and I did not expect it to be this intense. When I say intense, I mean in the respect of how God healed, tilled up, and dealt with every aspect of my faith during this time. It was not at all what I expected. It turned out to be one of the most painful yet sweetest times I spent with my mother in my fifty-five years of life.

So no matter what your relationship is with your loved one, God will use it in ways you could have never dreamed, if you allow it! I mean unfathomable to the human brain. The only comparison I can think of is how painful and sweet giving birth is to a new parent.

Our mother was a woman of small stature, but she ruled with the hand of a giant and walked with footsteps like thunder in time of correction. There was never any mistake what was headed your way, and the same mistake was never made twice! But those sounds echoed like the earth quaking when you messed with her family in any way, shape, or form, and those mistakes definitely did not happen twice!

Mom loved to be with all of the babies, and as she grew older, the firm correcting nature turned to softness and longing to see smiles, eyes to brighten, and hear the giggles of those she loved so dearly. And she went to every garage sale she could find looking for that toy that would bring the smiles and giggles. She loved to wear clothes of bright colors and hats of character that expressed her playful nature. She did not care what people thought, and she was always honest and up-front with all questions asked of her by family and friends. The one thing people knew about Ms. Betty was that if you did not want to know what she thought, you better not ask! But she was honest out of love because she believed that people did need to know the truth, and no one deserved a lie. She loved deeply those in her life and made all the hard decisions no matter the cost to her. As a mother, she hurt twice as bad as those who were hurting in her life, and that was a burden she gladly bore.

Mom was no stranger to hard times, and she was not afraid of facing them. She walked among the tallest and strongest, with her head held high with integrity, and her ability to work was as hard as any man without complaint.

She walked thousands of miles as a postal worker, and at the end of the day, tired as she was, she grabbed her lawn chair, loaded the children in the car, and away we went to every ball game and every drill team event we ever had in Kaufman, Texas. She never missed a game and was always the loudest cheerleader for her kids. And when the day was done and the lights were turned off at the ballfields, we went home for baths, and she finally laid her weary head down to rest long enough to start again the next day.

It is impossible to sum our mother's life up in one page. The crazy stories we have shared with one another and the tears we have shed will last a lifetime, and her legacy is huge. The countless people who have trailed through to say goodbye has been overwhelming, in the fact she affected so many lives outside of what we already knew about!

Mom had many names—Betty Boop, Momma, Grandma, crazy white Grandma, friend, and wife, but the name she most proud of was daughter of a king!

She and her loved ones were given a very special gift from the Lord, and that was the opportunity to say goodbye.

In her final days, she left very specific instructions for her family as she said her goodbyes here on earth—take care of each other, make sure you get together when you can but most importantly, I want to be with everyone one day. And she was not negotiating on that instruction. She wanted every man, woman, and child in her family to come to know Jesus as their Lord and Savior! She longed for that more than anything else. The one thing in this life she could not bear was if even one was left behind. Words only cheapen the intenseness of her pleas in her final moments as she squeezed the hand of her child, begging everyone to know how important this was to her.

Mom's life may have ended here, but no doubt she kicked up gold dust as she ran to her Savior in her new glorified body!

Prologue

Most women look forward to being mothers when they are little girls. They, then, become women and see their dreams turn into reality. From the moment you find out you're pregnant, the excitement is so intoxicating. You look at yourself in the mirror from the side and imagine how your belly will look at the ninth month. Anticipation is almost too much to bear. You can't wait for that belly to grow and the glow of pregnancy to set in. There is a real, little person growing inside of you.

And so, it begins. The morning sickness strikes hard! You just want to feel normal again and eat eggs, or have a hamburger without running to throw it up. As this stage continues, the stretching and hormonal roller coaster starts. You don't even mean to cry but then, suddenly do. Your husband looks at you as if you've lost your mind, and your tears become bigger. Now, you start to think, *Oh, great! He's sorry he married a crazy woman!*

Which then causes insecurity. You panic and start to think that not only are you crazy but that your belly will be huge before long, so he'll have a fat, crazy lady for a wife. Your tears are not enough anymore. The loud uncontrollable sobbing starts, and he starts running in circles around you to see what happened.

Now, the second trimester hits. By the end of it, you just want to eat at a restaurant where the restroom isn't ten miles from your table because you know you're going to have to pee at least thirty times before you even finish your meal.

You make it to the final stretch, the third trimester. If you're lucky, it's during the winter months so the heat from your body won't cause the paint to peel off the walls as you walk by. All the while, your husband, who is shivering like a blizzard, has hit your bedroom after he fell asleep because you've cranked the air down to fifty degrees! By the end of this trimester, you're so ready to be able to just shave your legs and be the master of your own bladder again. I won't even mention the granny panties you've been wearing. They're just not what you want to see in the laundry anymore!

The day has arrived. Either your water broke on its own or the doctor has taken pity on your husband and decided to induce you.

You make it to the hospital, and if you haven't already started experiencing labor pains, they're not far behind. The first one hits, and you think to yourself, *Well, that wasn't too terribly bad. I can do this!*

But by the third or fourth hour, you're over it, and you want *drugs!* The pain has now become exhausting, revolving, tightening, and loosening of all your muscles.

Finally, you get to hold this little one you have longed for since you were a little girl. The same little one who has used your bladder as a kick ball for the last nine months. The very minute you lay eyes on that tiny person, you suddenly forget the labor pains, the hot sweaty nights, the moods swings, and every uncomfortable thing you have gone through. All you see is perfection! You have a high that words only cheapen to try and explain! It's an instant, intense love, and feeling of purpose that cannot be duplicated by any drug or drink!

The beginning of life is painful, intense, and above all, one of the closest times you will come to hearing the voice of God. It's in the cry of that beautifully created little human and seeing His face in the perfection of your baby.

Saying hello for the first time is one of the hardest things a woman does in her life. It is also, for the father, one of the longest nine months for him. He shares the sympathy pains and emotions, whether women agree with that or not. The pain is indescribable, during and after. C-section or natural, it doesn't matter. It is the most intense experience you will ever have. The instant love is overwhelming and God-given.

But with that overwhelming love, is the pain that accompanied with it. Both love and pain last your entire life. That is the way it was intended.

Saying "hello" is sweet and painful. Saying "goodbye" can be just as sweet as it is painful. "Goodbye" is hard. I will never question that. But I will tell you, with my experience in this "goodbye" moment, I wouldn't have traded it for anything this world has to offer. It was painful, confusing, anger-provoking, and exhausting. Yet in the end, it was healing, peaceful, life-learning, and praise-filled.

Yes, it was all the above!

Remember the love and pain the new mother experienced? Well now, by transfer, you are the new parent of your parent. Where the new mother is in the "hello" stage, you begin your journey of the "goodbye" stage. As harsh as that sounds, it is a fact that is supported all throughout scripture. The best example is Ecclesiastics 3:1–8, for example.

> To everything there is a season, A time for every purpose under heaven; A time to be born, And a time to die; A time to plant, And a time to pluck what is planted; A time to kill, And a time to heal; A time to break down, And a time to build up; A time to weep, And a time to laugh; A time to mourn, And a time to dance; A time to cast away stones, And a time to gather stones; A time to embrace, And a time to refrain from embracing; A time to gain, And a time to lose; A time to keep, And a time to throw away; A time to tear, And a time to sew; A time to keep silence, And a time to speak; A time to love, And a time to hate; A time of war, And a time of peace.

I believe Solomon is simply describing life as it is. There are fourteen different contrasts here, and it is simply written that there is a time for everything in life. Here is the largest point to be made; remember with Solomon's writings, that in all things, there seems to be balance—giving and taking, gaining and losing. Part of his reasoning is that in the overall scheme of human life, apart from God, is "meaningless."

I hope as you read about the experiences I had with my mother in the last few days of her life, it will warm your heart, give you peace, and let you know that it's okay to say goodbye and still have pain, love, and peace all at once. Most would say I was crazy, but I say I was given a gift that no gold or silver could ever buy.

Chapter 1

Facing the Decision Day

What do you do when the one whom you were, at one time, most dependent on; becomes the dependent? I had been noticing changes in Momma for a while. She was slowing down, it seemed. Now, you must understand that slowing down for Mom was regular speed for a normal person.

In December of 2014, she suffered a massive heart attack. It left her with only 33 percent capacity of function in her heart. My sister was staying with her at that time, and I cringe to think what would've happened had she not been there. She had to have a pacemaker and defibrillator put in.

Mom had gone through several life-changing events in a few short years. Her current husband had fallen sick. He still lived in Missouri at the time, and she had moved back to Texas in 2010 to be closer to her family.

She went back to Missouri to be with him in his final days. He died, which then caused depression, along with a situation that transpired while she was there. I don't know what happened, but I do know that it did a number on her mental state. The depression was the beginning stage of her not eating correctly. She was hospitalized for a brief period because of this and went home.

Eventually, she reached a point where she had to stay with my younger brother and his wife. They got her back up on her feet, good enough to go back to her own house.

Mom was seventy-two to seventy-seven years old when all of this, and much more, happened back-to-back. Not only did she have health problems, but she tended to take on worries about her adult children that only exacerbated her health conditions. She started falling and calling for help to get up. One time, she fell in a way that she couldn't reach her phone. Sadly, she laid there for quite a while before we finally found her. I spoke with my siblings about checking into an assisted living, but they just did not feel she was ready for that yet.

She was always so mobile and strong in her convictions, but at this point, she started second guessing herself and her decisions. She was no longer the "enforcer" but was wondering if all the choices she made in the past were good ones. Instead of letting her adult children and grandchildren learn from their mistakes, she was now the "enabler." That was something she said she would never do. It is not good for a person on a fixed income.

Not only had I seen these changes in her thoughts but also her driving ability. I noticed dents on her car and observed that her reaction times were seriously delayed. She wasn't eating and losing weight again. My niece, who was a nurse, began to notice the obvious changes as well.

I asked my brother, who spoke to my mother every morning, and sister, who often went by in the evenings, if they had noticed any changes in her. Neither had yet, but to me, it was becoming obvious that all was not as it had once been.

So where do you go from here? How do you take someone who was so independent her whole life and start putting restrictions on her? Do you move her in with you? Possibly. If you have the room and ability to take care of an elderly person. If not, some hard choices have to be made. And if you're the one that has to make them, you're the one that will take on the burden that is like that of a new parent.

In June of 2019, Mom landed in the hospital due to being really confused, disoriented, and running a fever. She had lost so much weight that I was afraid she was seriously malnourished. I also realized that she couldn't hear me very well, and I had to keep repeating myself. At first, I just marked it up to the confusion, but later, she told me that a soft drink can exploded in the box next to her chair.

My husband, Bubba, and I went to her house later that day. Sure enough, there was a can that was split from the top to the bottom. He said it must have sounded like a bomb going off the way the can looked.

I let her doctor know the next day. He explained what all the tests showed, which was a laundry list of issues. He did say that if the can exploded, it could have caused a brain injury. That would explain a lot of what she was currently experiencing. The confusion, difficulty learning and retaining new information, trouble speaking coherently, unsteadiness, and problems with hearing or vision. The way he explained it was like that of a battlefield explosion, and the shock waves affecting the brain.

He said that if it were a mild one, we would see improvements but that it could set Alzheimer's into motion. If that were indeed the case, we would start to see subtle changes in her, and they would worsen over time. She was never the same again.

From the hospital, she was sent for a stay in a rehab. Once again, I approached the topic of assisted living, and everyone agreed. This way, she could still be independent but have around the clock assistance if needed.

Soon after, we went and toured a facility to make sure it was clean and see what type of care the people there were getting. We liked it, and it was nice that Mom would have her own little room like an apartment. There were social activities (Mom was an extremely social person) so that was great. All the rooms were decorated cute, and they ate in a dining room together, which, again, was great. They would come in and clean once a week, do her laundry, and even distribute her medicines if we needed them to.

When the rehab gave us an approximate discharge date, we moved all of Mom's things into her little apartment. I went and bought all new curtains, toiletries, and a bed spread. My sister brought some décor. Jeff bought her a love seat for guests. We had her all set up and even took her car and parked it where she could have it there, should she be able to drive again.

October 2019 came. I dreaded this day, more than going to the dentist to have all my teeth pulled without any pain medication. This was the hardest thing I can remember, doing up to this point with my mom. We had to tell her she was not going home but that we had moved her to this little apartment.

To say she was not happy is a huge understatement! She felt like we put her in Alcatraz, so we could forget about her! The fight was on.

She pouted, she argued, and she blamed all the women in her life—my sister, my sister-in-law, and I! Her boys just would *not* have done this to her. All I heard for the first few weeks was that the women there did not like her, the meals were horrible, they wouldn't let her eat, and so forth.

I knew I would withstand the worst of her anger, and sure enough, I did. But I had no choice other than to take it. I did love my momma, despite what she thought. None of us could quit our jobs, move her in, and take care of her the way she needed. But that did not stop the guilt I carried over this.

The one thing I had learned in fifty-five years was that my brothers were the embodiment of perfection in her eyes.

Don't get me wrong, I knew my mother loved me. She was just really proud of her boys, especially her youngest one. "Ole Rotten Jeff" as I refer to him. He sat on her lap as she fed him Malt-O-Meal until he was sixteen, it seemed like. We still tease him to this day about that. His response is always, "Don't hate me because I was perfect." Again, we all just laugh and let him think that!

As I am writing this though, there are several things that come to mind. I did not always appreciate my mom the way I should have. So she was not totally to blame for the way she felt. My brothers always made a fuss over her. When a man, son or not, gave her positive attention, that always made her feel special. Most of the men in Mom's life did not treat her like she should've been treated. She was always much better to them than they were to her.

When I would visit her, I could tell she was really happy to see Bubba but not so happy I came with him. She adored my husband and often let me know how much I didn't deserve him.

When her great-grandchildren came to see her, it made her whole week! Particularly her youngest grandson, Camden. She was really obsessed with that little guy. And why wouldn't she be? He was this little curly headed, loving baby that allowed her to love all over him and not once try to get away. And most of all, he loved her right back!

Chapter 2

Life in Assisted Living

Eventually, Mom settled in and started attending exercise sessions, bingo, and other little things they had going. She made a few friends, and everyone knew that Ms. Betty loved to talk, so she did to anyone that would listen.

She handed out candy to all the little ones on Halloween that came through a couple of weeks after she got there. Needless to say, she loved it. I took a big bag of candy to her, so she could load up their little baskets.

My siblings and I tried to see her as often as we could. My sister would take Mom grilled cheese sandwiches and watch some of their shows at night together. I would go by after work and take her things she would ask for. My brothers would go when they could, and man, that was like Christmas to her!

Bingo was her thing. She would take all the things she won and put them to the side. When we came to visit, she would load us up with them. But she saved all the cookies and candies for Camden. The longer Mom was there, the more she began to like it. By the end of the year, which was only a few months, she had settled down.

I tried to call Mom as much as I could, and she eventually came to realize I was not the horrible daughter she thought I was. She finally got to a point where she would call me through the day and even started hugging me again when I came to see her. She would even show me how good she had gotten at her exercises.

Jeff called Mom every day, and it became their ritual. But if he missed a day, that was his wife's fault. I always laughed inside when Mom would tell me that. She thought that because his wife, Tina, would tease Jeff about being a "Momma's boy." Mom simply didn't like the fact that Jeff had another woman in his life that was as important as she was. "Ole Rotten Jeff" was supposed to be all Mom's, and she didn't like sharing. That always made me laugh.

I do have to say, there were perks to not being her favorite. Mom lost the ability to filter her words and thoughts, which is common among older people. Most, but not all, elderly people become obsessed about their bathroom habits.

One time, Jeff, Bubba, and I were visiting on a Saturday. Completely out of nowhere, my mother went into a story about her being constipated and then finally passing the "biggest poop she has ever seen."

Now, the best part of Mom getting on one of these topics was watching the faces of the men in the room! I cannot tell you how funny it was to watch them try to avoid eye contact with anyone else, or just simply act like they couldn't hear her. It was like they were thinking, *If I don't move, she won't notice I'm here!*

I would laugh until I cried because Mom was going to be heard one way or another, and she was going to call on someone to validate her story! *No one* wanted to be picked for that task!

On this particular occasion, Mom actually saved her poop in the toilet! Yep, you read that right. She saved it because she didn't think anyone would believe her when she told them how big it was. She looked at Jeff and said, "Jeff it's still in there. Go look at it. It will blow your mind at how big it is!"

I could tell by the look on his face that he was mortified, which only made it that much funnier. I had my hand over my face laughing so hard, finding it hard to breathe.

Bubba just sat there on the love seat, acting like he didn't hear a thing. Trying to find anyone else to do it, Jeff looked at Bubba and said, "Go on, Bubba. You're closer."

Bubba never looked up from his phone and said with a dry reply, "Nope, she is *your* momma."

Now, I was in full blown hysteria with laughing. Jeff looked at me with a crooked smile, trying his best not to bust out laughing himself. Catching my breath, just long enough, I said, "There is definitely perks to not being the favorite child," and I resumed laughing uncontrollably.

My mom just sat there smiling, knowing she had embarrassed everyone. I think she was just a little tickled at herself.

This is just one of the many stories about Momma in her last years, that when I think about them, I still laugh just as hard as I did the day they happened. My momma was a real character. She could make me laugh at all her antics.

Her birthday was coming up in mid-February of 2020. In talking with my niece one night, she said it would be great if we could do something special for her birthday. We decided to surprise her with a party. I called everyone in the family and let them know that I booked a room at a local restaurant, on the Friday before, as a surprise for Mom. I ordered her cake, and on this cake, I put a picture of when she was a young girl on it. She was always so proud of the way she looked when she met my dad. He called her, "Betty Boop." So naturally her cake had the cartoon *Betty Boop* with her picture right beside it.

She had been in and out of doctor appointments, so that was the perfect excuse to pick her up. I told her that we had a late appointment and to be ready when I got there. Sure enough, when I got there, she was sitting at the door with her walker. I got her loaded up and off we went. While I was driving, I got a phone call and acted like the doctor's office just canceled. I told her while we were out, we might as well get a bite to eat. At first, she said she just wasn't up to it, but I said it would do her some good to get out a little.

We arrived at the restaurant. I got her walker out and in we went. I motioned to the hostess that we were with the party in the back, and she just nodded to go on. I led Mom to the room, and when she entered, everyone yelled "Surprise!"

The room was packed! I was shocked when Mom turned her walker around and started to leave. I asked, "Where are you going?"

She replied, "Well, someone is having a party in there, so we don't need to go in."

I just busted out laughing and said, "Momma, that party is for you! Look around, it's all your family!" She then turned around and started looking at all the faces and realized it was her family.

I cannot express how my heart was feeling in that moment. I had mixed emotions. I was a little sad that she didn't realize we would do that for her. Then, I was warmed by the biggest smile I had seen in years that covered her frail face.

I couldn't have been prouder of my family at that point! Over thirty members showed up for this event for my mom! When she saw the cake, she was tickled with it. Naturally, I made sure Camden was sitting next to Mom along with some of her great-grandchildren.

This was one of the proudest moments in my mother's life. After the party and before anyone left, I got everyone to gather around my mom and had a waiter take our picture. I later had this blown up into a seventeen by eighteen picture and framed, so she could hang it on her wall in her little apartment. I also made her a photo album of all the pictures I took that night. She carried that little book in her basket on her walker and showed it off every chance she got. And when the rehab nurses came in, she explained who everyone was in the picture on the wall. She was indeed proud of her family!

But as always, life gets busier, and the visits became less and less. I knew Mom was being taken care of, and I just got too comfortable with that fact. She was also beginning a social life there at the assisted living facility. Mom was tired at the end of the day a lot of times when I talked to her, so it made it easier on me to feel a little less guilty. Not only myself but all of us. Before, Mom would just hop in the car and come to see us, but now, she depended solely on us to come to her. Still today, my biggest regret is that I didn't go to see her more when I had the chance. Trust me, it will haunt you for a while after you lose your parent. So don't make the same mistake I made. Cherish what you have while you have it. You never know what is waiting right around the corner, which would affect them and yourself as well.

Rumors of a pandemic were in the air, and the television was buzzing with the news of the Coronavirus, aka COVID-19. Little did we know, this would be a complete game changer.

Chapter 3

Isolation

I'm so glad we did my mother's birthday party before COVD-19 consumed the United States in complete panic and mayhem. God was so good in the fact He planted that thought. I am simply not that good by myself to pull that off alone.

When we threw Mom's party, her facility hadn't gone on lockdown yet. Many other nursing homes and assisted living agencies had, which meant no visitors were allowed in, and patients were not allowed out. If you wanted to be able to spend that time with your loved one, then you had to take them home with you to stay. No one could have predicted the impact this nasty pandemic would have, not only physically but emotionally on our elderly parents.

I was at church on Sunday when I got a call from Mom's nurse at the assisted living facility. He said she had fallen and hit her head. She wasn't making any sense when he would ask her simple questions. He decided to have her taken to Baylor in Dallas for head trauma. I left and headed straight there to meet her at the hospital.

At the time, COVID-19 precautions were in full force at hospitals. Only one person was allowed in at a time. Your temperature was taken, you were asked a series of questions before being allowed in, and face masks were required at all times. After finishing the gauntlet of exercises to protect the innocent, I found her in her ER room.

She was confused with what was going on. She felt warm to me, and she was shivering. The knot on her head, that they thought she got from the fall, was from her childhood. It had been there her whole life. I let the nurse, that was attending to her, know that her confusion was not from that knot on her head. Mom was, however, pale and looked like she just didn't feel good.

I had only been there for about an hour when a nurse came into the room. She told me to get out now, leave the building, and said they would call me with updates. I got a little bit of an attitude with her and asked, "Exactly why do I have to leave?"

She informed me that I was in a COVID-19 unit and should not be there.

I complied and left the room. Bubba was waiting in the truck and was a bit surprised I showed up so fast. He was settled in for a long night in the truck. We stayed about another hour. Realizing they were not going to let me back in, we headed back home.

I made several calls that night, to try to find out if the doctor had been in to see her yet. Their response was always the same, "We are waiting on all of the test results to come back."

Finally, the next morning, I received a call from a young doctor at Baylor. He said that Mom's X-rays showed COVID-19 signs, and she was being put in quarantine. I was shocked! When I got off the phone, I sat there stunned. After a minute or two, Bubba looked at me and said, "Well?"

He was just as stunned.

The first thing I did was call Mom's living facility, to tell them she was showing COVID-19 signs. The administrator told me that representatives of the Texas Health Department had just showed up there. They were threatening to shut the doors of that place because they had yet to comply with the CDC guidelines. I guess news of Mom had traveled faster to the state than to her family.

Up to this point, Mom's place was still allowing visitors. They knew the impact it would have on their patients if they had to be isolated from family and friends. They loved their little people and didn't want them to be put in that position until it was absolutely necessary. Well, the time had come; the doors were being locked. Masks were required for staff and patients. And eventually, these people were quarantined to their rooms, which only made it worse!

Mom was in the hospital for eight weeks, and she was furious with me for that. She would call, wanting out every day, and her depression came back.

When she finally got to go back to her facility, she was quarantined another two weeks to her room with no one in or out! After she got out of lockdown from being in the hospital, she would not even let me take her to her follow-up appointment. If she left her facility, that meant she would be quarantined again when she came back.

We did get to see her through the doors at her place from time to time, but that had to be scheduled. A few times, they even let her come outside, only if everyone was wearing mask and stayed six feet apart. It got to a point where I had to ship her supplies, butter pecan boost, diapers, and things like that through Amazon.

I can't even imagine what life was like for Mom from March to December of 2020. It had to be one of the loneliest times in her life. It seemed like the patients were quarantined to their rooms more than they were allowed out. I had to keep calling the nurses there to go turn Mom's phone back on. She would either let it die, or she would accidentally turn the volume down to where she couldn't hear it ring. Thankfully, they were always so gracious in helping me out with things like that.

Finally, I called and asked if Mom could come to our Christmas with my kids and not have to go into quarantine when she returned. Surprisingly enough, they said she could. Mom was so excited. She was finally going to get to touch and talk to some of her family face-to-face. She even got to hold one of her new great-grandsons.

I picked her up at 5:00 PM on Christmas Eve. She came with me to my youngest son's house for cookie baking, opening of gifts, and the game "Silly Santa." She won an electric lap blanket. She hugged on my granddaughters and told them what beautiful babies they were. This was a very treasured time for all of us. I watched as my daughters-in-law did everything they could to make Mom feel at home. Jeff came to see her as well, and she was talking everyone's ear off the entire time. All my kids just sat and visited with her, and she loved it.

I couldn't help but notice how frail she was starting to look. Mom was one of the strongest forces in our lives, growing up, and it hurt my heart deeply to know that time would take her one day. Life will smack you right in the face sometimes, and this was one of those times.

Something deep inside of me was saying, "Pay attention!" I will always believe that the Holy Spirit was prompting every movement during that Christmas. I would catch myself watching her as she played with the kids and talked to my boys. She enjoyed watching the little ones with their new toys and presents. I even bought everyone a gift from her. She always made it a point to make sure she spent $10 on the little kids until they turned twelve.

Whenever I've looked back on my mom's life, there were times that I felt like she didn't desire a relationship with my family, the way she did with my sister's and brothers' family. If I were honest, I was always jealous of this, but this Christmas, she was with us. And that was the best gift I could have ever received.

Despite what the past held, my heart was longing for more time with Mom. The pictures taken that night make my heart feel like it's wrapped in a soft warm blanket and held in time. I am amazed at how God is so precise in His timing. I couldn't have possibly understood what that night would come to mean to me and my family later.

I am so immensely proud of my kids, nieces, and nephews. They all loved my mom. My mom was hard on all the females in our family. It would take the final days of my mother's life, and the entering in of God's ability for the heart to hear, for me to understand why that was.

I love that night now more than I did during the actual event itself. It's hard to understand how that is, but I realized, all good things come through God. I'm still amazed by how a nobody like me can be loved like He loved on me throughout all of this.

Chapter 4

The Final Battle Begins

January 20, 2021, was my father's birth date. He would have been 102. Sitting at my desk that day, I was amazed that he would have been that old.

Around 2:00 PM, I got a call from Mom's nurse. He told me he was almost certain that Mom had broken her hip. My heart jumped into my throat, and a sudden nausea hit. He informed me that he was 99 percent sure because of the preliminary exam he gave her and based on the way her leg was lying to the side. He said she only complained of pain when she had to move it a certain way.

COVID precautions were still in place, and I knew if she left before I got there, I may not get to see her again if she had to have surgery. I asked him if he could wait until I got there to call the ambulance, and he said he would. I know he must have thought I was cruel for wanting him to wait, but I wanted to see her before she left.

We got to her place in record time. I went in, and she was in her recliner, just like nothing was wrong. I asked her if she hurt, and she said only when she moved her foot. I told him to go ahead and call the ambulance. I could also tell the way her leg was laying, that the hip was broken. I was trying not to cry or get upset, so I just sat quietly waiting. I text my siblings to let them know what was happening.

I stayed until the ambulance got there. I made sure she had her phone, charger, and told her I loved her. They loaded her up in the ambulance, and Bubba asked me if we were going to the hospital. I sat there and had to think about this. Hospitals were still inundated with COVID patients, and he was on a mild chemotherapy medication, for a condition he had been diagnosed with recently. I knew they weren't going to let me in right away with Mom, so I just told him, "We can go to the house. They have my number and know to call me right away."

The guilt was overwhelming for not going up there. It was like I was sending her away, and no one cared about her. My heart was crying out for a break from all the pain I had been going through over the past few years. Not that I was not alone in all of this. My siblings did help when I couldn't be there. Jeff was vigilant about calling Mom, as much and as often as he could, and seeing her when he was in off the road.

What I haven't said yet is what was going on behind the scenes at my house during this whole time. From transitioning my mother into her new environment, all the way through her hip breaking.

I had to have surgery to remove a lap band I had done in 2007, and it was not pleasant to say the least. It made a mess of my stomach, and part of it had to be removed. That was in October of 2019, right after we moved Mom into her apartment.

In December of 2019, I let my doctor talk me into a surgery, due to my shoulders deteriorating. That surgery went south fast. They ended up having to remove all my sutures, and they left exceptionally large open wounds that were six to seven inches long for five days, trying to get my circulation back.

My poor husband had to change the bandages. His hands shook, and sweat broke out on his forehead. He was so terrified, and I didn't understand why until later. The doctor made my husband send him pictures to prevent us from having to take the painful trip to Dallas everyday just for him to see how it was looking. Unfortunately, that didn't work. About a week later, the doctor decided that he would just close the incisions, and let the chips fall where they may. Well, they fell like a plane loaded with solid lead to the ground at warp speed. It left me seriously disfigured.

One day, I decided to look for the pictures myself, and it was then that I finally saw what he saw. I was totally humiliated by it and hid in the bathroom that night, crying like a baby as he slept.

But as He always does, God showed up and gave me comfort and peace, and I moved onto the next thing.

Early that next year, my husband, who is my everything, was diagnosed with primary myelofibrosis. I was petrified that I would lose him. If you or a loved one is ever diagnosed with something, do yourself a favor and do not "Google" it! I was having panic attacks and hid from everyone when they would hit. I didn't want to add any stress to him. That was, until one day, he came in the house, and I was right in the middle of one, and the look on his face was pure terror!

You see, when I would have one of these attacks, I could not breathe. I would sweat like crazy, I couldn't speak, and my mind was out of control! Most of the time, I had to pray like a madwoman to make it stop. For someone who had never experienced seeing this, I am sure he thought someone had just died. Hence, the reason I would hide when they hit. Yet he just came in, grabbed me, and held me until I calmed down, and we talked about it all. We prayed together that night, and I haven't had one since. Bubba's numbers continue to improve with each visit, and his doctor assures me that Bubba will live a long happy life. I praise God for that!

That taught me a big lesson. Satan wants things hidden and not brought to the light, so he can use them to torment you.

Now, I faced yet another battle. I knew that a broken hip was really a terrible thing for an elderly person. Her doctor called me when he finally got everything set up, and he made me feel a lot better about it. He said he had done a surgery on an eighty-three-year-old man, and that man bounced right back and was still active today. He did say she would have to put in some work. He told me that she was relatively healthy and should be able to handle this surgery just fine, so I consented on all the forms, and they scheduled surgery for the next day.

I called to check on Mom the next day. They said she was seriously confused and would be for a few days. They advised me to give her a few days to get reoriented. I called twice a day to check on her. Each day, they told me she was doing better and better.

Her social caseworker called me and asked if there was a rehab I had in mind to send her to. I called others in the family, and we agreed that maybe if she were in Terrell, more people might visit her. Her last rehab was in Rowlett, and some complained it was too far.

In the end, the decision was made to send her to a Terrell rehab. Once again, she was quarantined for two weeks, but they did let me go once while she was in quarantine to see her. I was a little perturbed because she didn't even have a TV in her room. Just her, all by herself. She was alone and confused, and I'm sure she felt totally abandoned. That should've been a clue to what the quality of that facility really was.

I asked for her rehab schedule, which I never received. Then, I got a call from her nurse there, informing me she was starting to develop pressure wounds on her heels and the top of her toes.

I am no doctor, but if she is up and moving like the doctor ordered, this wouldn't be happening.

I went a couple of times after quarantine, and her roommate sure had a lot to say about Mom's rehab. She let me know that they weren't doing what they were supposed to be. It had been five weeks at this point, and Mom had not even been back to the surgeon to have her staples removed. I kept calling, and all they had was one excuse after another for that not happening.

I could not take her due to COVID. Finally, her doctor's office called me furious and let me know Mom had missed two appointments. I called the facility and spoke with the administrator, who assured me Mom would make her Friday appointment.

Well, she made it to her appointment all right! That doctor called, chewing me up one side, and back down the other for having Mom in that place! I explained I was having her moved that night. I then called her other rehab in Rowlett, and they made arrangements to have Mom moved there. The administrator of the Terrell facility assured me they would have her ready.

At 9:00 PM, I received a phone call from the Rowlett coordinator. She said when they went to pick Mom up, the person at the door told them that Mom passed away and wasn't there. I could feel the heat start at my feet, and by the time it reached my head, I was in complete rage.

I called the Terrell administrator and said, "If my mother isn't at the new facility before midnight, I will be up there first thing in the morning with an escort to press charges on you and your facility."

I added, "And you better not bill my mother's insurance for the transport either."

She said she would take care of it but then proceeded to tell me she would call me the next day to discuss my mother's bill.

I told her I would put it on the calendar and be there at her office. She said she would rather do it over the phone. I quickly replied, "No, ma'am. I'm going to sit across the desk from you while you *try* to tell me how much I owe you. That way you can see the look in my eye when I tell you that you will not receive a dime from my mother or her insurance."

I continued with, "And I will promise you one thing. If I receive a bill, or if the insurance receives a bill, I will retain a third-party representative to sue you and your care unit for the damages made to my mother, documented by her doctor, that were due to neglect on your part."

My mother landed in Rowlett at 11:00 PM that night. I never received a bill, and as far as I know, her insurance wasn't billed either.

Your parents are people, not cattle to be ran through a sale barn to the highest bidder until they serve no purpose. They have rights! Protect their rights to be treated like human beings and not gum on the bottom of someone's shoes!

The pressure wounds on her heels were worse than they originally said. That is never a good thing. Even after my mom went to the new unit in Rowlett, the wounds continued to worsen. That made rehab difficult because it was so incredibly painful for Mom to walk with those wounds.

During the next few months, Mom was up and down in her health. She was not progressing like she should've been in her rehab. I tried to see Mom after work at least twice a week, and I kept a photo journal of her. I took pictures of medications they were giving her through an IV and pictures of her heels. I was constantly sending them to my niece and asking questions. It wasn't hard to see that Mom was steadily going down.

One day, in late March of 2021, I went to see her. I had not been in a few extra days due to being sick and not wanting to risk her health. As soon as I walked into her room, I knew what was happening. I will never forget that day. I could feel a shifting in her spirit.

I face-timed some of my family so they could see her as well. Only a couple of them knew in their heart what was beginning to happen.

Mom didn't have many visitors up to that point. But after family members seeing that, she had several. Too bad it didn't last. Life gets busy for everyone. Even with the best intentions, we miss the mark. Her spirit was finally defeated, and I could physically feel it. I knew from that day where we were headed to. Even though it was hard, I did what I always do and pushed those feelings back.

Mom's allotted days on insurance had run out, and it was time to transition to the nursing home side. She was bedridden by that point, and the pressure wounds were much worse.

On one occasion, we had to get a nurse because Mom would not talk to me or open her eyes. I uncovered her feet, and one was swollen and red. They immediately started her on antibiotics through an IV. By the next day, she was joking and cutting up with Jeff. I made it a point to take pictures that day. She was sticking her tongue out at him, and it was hilarious. I was relieved to say the least!

The unit that Mom was in was full of good people who really cared. I never doubted them or their ability to take care of her. I just knew I had a responsibility to check on her.

Chapter 5

What Does This Mean?

Mom had a doctor's appointment, and I was meeting her there. The facility called me the night before to give me the address in Rockwall, to where she was going. She was going to a vascular doctor and was being sent there because of the pressure wounds. They just simply could not get the skin to start healing, and it was suspected that a lack of circulation could be causing it.

This was on a Thursday, and I hadn't seen her all week. Once again, I had been sick with strep throat and wanted to make sure I didn't see her until I was over it.

Bubba and I took off half a day of work and planned to meet her there. We arrived at the address but couldn't find her doctor's office. Finally, after searching every floor, I called the office to ask them what floor they were on. Their answer threw me off because the building she said she was in was at Baylor of Dallas. I decided it would be better to make sure my mother really had an appointment there.

When I told her my mother's name, the receptionist was so tickled. She said she knew my mother from her first stay at Rowlett. She went on to tell me how much she loved my mom.

You never know how much your parents touch the lives of others until a total stranger shows you. I was very warmed by her words. It was also a reflection of the genuineness of the workers at the Rowlett facility.

I told the doctor's receptionist that I was in Rockwall, and that it wouldn't be possible for me to make it in time for her appointment. I asked her to have the doctor call me when my mother arrived and she said, "Oh yes! This is one of the best doctors you will ever meet, and he will call you!"

We grabbed a quick lunch and headed back to work. I wanted to save my vacation time in case there was an emergency later down the road with Mom. How could I have possibly known how close that time was?

Thirty minutes later, I received another call from the vascular doctor's office. Mom still hadn't arrived, which meant she was thirty minutes late. This concerned me a great deal. My first phone call was to her facility. One of the ladies in the administrative office looked at the schedule and said, "She is headed to a doctor's appointment." When I told her Mom had not arrived, she said, "Give me a minute, and I will call you back."

About ten minutes passed and she finally called back. Mom was still in her room, and I could hear a lot of commotion going on in the background. There was a nurse telling the administrative clerk to hand him the phone. I heard him say that he needed to talk to me because it was urgent. My stomach sunk to the bottom of my feet and panic struck.

He got on the phone and proceeded to tell me that he had to call an ambulance to come pick up Mom. Her feet were bad, he was not liking the way they looked at all, and she was starting to contract a fever.

Mom was already so frail, and her condition was making her deteriorate so quickly, that I was overly anxious after this call. Once again, I told them to transport her and have the hospital call me when she arrived. That was the longest hour and a half I had in a long time.

Finally, I decided to call the hospital myself and ask, "Has the doctor seen her yet?" Mom's attending nurse got on the phone. She told me I really needed to come up there and said we had a lot to talk about. She also wanted me to see Mom's feet. At this point, all I knew was I did not want to see her wounds! I just did not think I could do it. Nausea hit again, but I stopped and told myself, "You can do this! It is not about you!" I said a quick prayer, and we left to go to the hospital.

By the time we got there, they already had a room assigned to Mom. With all the COVID restrictions, we weren't allowed in the ER. They instructed us to go up to the second floor to wait and said she would be up there shortly.

We went on up and sat in the waiting room facing the hallway, hoping we would see when they brought her in. After about twenty minutes, they passed by with Mom in a bed. My heart was struck with a sudden stabbing pain as she was wheeled by. It was so hard to believe that that small little human in the bed passing by us was my mother!

My mother worked for the post office for over forty years and walked more miles than most people walk their entire life. She carried a mailbag that weighed more than thirty pounds, at times. Her work ethic was impeccable. Not to mention, she worked circles around the men she worked with. She was small in stature but always stood tall and was powerful in motion. My mind was reeling as I sat in tearful heartache, feeling so helpless at this point.

They took Mom to her room. As we started to walk in behind them, they stopped us at the door. The nurse told me that they wanted to get her cleaned up before we went in. She also said they needed to document the wounds and get wound care to come in and evaluate her.

I ask them if they would take pictures from my phone of the wounds because I was keeping a photo journal of Mom. They told me I could come in and do it myself. I guess the look on my face must have spoken a thousand words. She looked at me and asked, "Would you like for me to do it for you?"

I said, "I think that would be better. Thank you for doing that for me."

I was extremely impressed at how compassionate the staff was there at the hospital. The smell coming from Mom's room was horrible. We had our masks on, yet it wasn't stopping it from being overwhelming.

She took the pictures and brought my phone back to me. Bubba looked at them and put them in the "hidden" folder on my phone. I could tell by the look on his face that it wasn't good.

We had already been through wound care issues with his mother. She always bounced right back, so that gave me some hope for a brief moment. I just kept thinking this was just a setback. Nothing to get all worked up over.

After they had changed my mom's clothes and removed her bandages, they told us we could come in. I didn't know her feet would be uncovered. Bubba stepped in first and immediately turned around and said, "Look at the floor until you get around to the other side."

I did just what he said. He knew me better than anyone. He knew I would lose it if I saw her feet. He could tell I was already having a challenging time keeping it together.

I got face-to-face with her and said, "Momma, I'm here. I'm sorry you feel so bad. They're going to get this taken care of now."

Tears began to stream down my face. She just opened her eyes and looked at me expressionless. My heart was screaming!

I turned around to see the wound care PA walking in, and we were asked to step out once again. We stepped into the hallway to wait. What I assumed was another doctor went in shortly after. She was a very petite lady, wearing a long white coat.

The doctor exited the room a short while later, and a nurse motioned for us to come in. The wound care PA was still in the room and had wrapped Mom's feet.

The first question she asked was, "How aggressive do you want us to be with her treatment?"

I just stood there, dumbfounded by the question. I replied, "I want you to do what needs to be done! I don't even understand why you're asking me how aggressive I want you to be?"

I did not like this lady, to say the least. She was abrasive and acted calloused to the fact that someone's mother was in there. She went on to say, "I don't think your mother can handle the type of surgeries it is going to take to fix this. She is in extremely poor health. I would recommend just sustaining the wounds."

At this point, I was picturing myself choking out this woman. I was becoming more infuriated with her tone and demeanor.

She was only rescued by a nurse walking up to me and handing me a phone. She told me it was the doctor with Mom's test results and said she wanted to talk to me. It was a good thing the nurse walked up at that time because the wound care PA was in danger, at that point, of getting knocked out!

I answered the phone, and the doctor was very compassionate with our conversation. She started with, "I am going to be very honest with you. Your mom is not good at all. She has sepsis, and her overall health is just poor. I do not recommend any surgeries to the feet. We will help your mom get comfortable tonight and talk more later. Hang in there, okay?"

The wound care PA started babbling as soon as I handed the phone back to the nurse. I just threw my hand up and said very bluntly, "Just sustain the wounds!"

I walked off with tears streaming down my face, not being able to control them. God bless Bubba because he sat with Mom, so I could fall apart without her seeing it.

I walked down to the waiting room and tried to calm down. I had to let all this sink in and try to understand what it all meant. *Should I call my family? Is this life threatening? Could she bounce back like Bubba's mother did? What exactly is happening, and how can I know what to do?*

But my heart knew what was happening. The heart is an amazing thing. The Spirit of God is so gentle when He speaks to you in such painful times. But if you listen and let Him, He guides your every step.

I said a short prayer and realized that, at this point, I had to call Jeff. He was on the road and a long distance from home. I didn't exactly know where he was, but I just knew he needed to head back. I did my best to collect myself. I dialed his number, and as soon as I heard his voice, I started shaking all over again.

I told him what the doctor said and added, "I really think you need to come home. It's different this time." By the time I was finished talking, I was a wreck again.

He replied, "Go get yourself calmed down, and I will work my way home. Let me know if you hear anything else."

I told him I would try to video call him from Bubba's phone, so he could talk to Mom.

I knew he would try to drive as far as he could and take as few naps as possible to get there. He was in Montana, and we were in Texas. But he was Momma's baby, and they had a special connection. He was going to fight hell itself, if he had to, just to get to her.

I called my sister, but her phone went to voice mail, so I called her son, Kris, and daughter, Tracey. I asked them to call everyone.

As always, they came through for me. Bubba called our kids to give them an update on Mom, and let them know how sick she really was.

Later that night, after we got home, Bubba told me about earlier that day, when he sat with Momma. He said she looked at him and asked, "Bubba, are we doing the right thing?"

He just answered her with, "Yes, Betty, I think we are doing the right thing for now."

Chapter 6

Making Her Comfortable

It seemed like the time that day slowed down to a crawl. I had one more call to make, and it was one I was dreading. I had been tiptoeing around it for about three months. I needed to call my Aunt Patsy. She was my mother's only living sibling. I love that crazy lady. The thought of having to tell her how sick Mom was, made me physically ill. I decided to call her daughter, and let her decide when and how to tell her.

Before Mom went to the assisted living, she and Patsy spoke every night. Patsy would tell Mom about her life, and Mom would tell her what she was doing wrong. I used to just laugh at those two. They fussed, but they just loved talking to each other.

As a kid, I loved when my aunts would visit. They were all so different and funny! Mom and my Aunt Loreen were, by far, the most outspoken. Patsy and Aunt Katherine would just sit and laugh at them. They used to argue playfully over who was right on any topic discussed. Those are some of my fondest memories growing up.

At times, it even seemed like they spoke a different language. They called cokes, "pop." Instead of saying "you all," they would say "you'ins." They didn't "wash" clothes, they "warshed" clothes. I would just giggle and giggle at the way they talked. As I got older, I would make fun of them. Aunt Patsy would try to pinch me and say, "Stop it, you ole' ornery thang you!" Now, she says that to my kids because they picked up where I left off!

I went back into Mom's room and sat down next to her. The smell was worse than ever before. I asked Bubba if he would come and say a prayer over Mom. I just didn't have it in me to do it myself without losing it.

He did without hesitation. It was a sweet prayer, and I even begin to calm a little. My heart was still aching, but the Lord was in that room with us, I could feel it. Trust me when I say that the only thing sustaining me was His presence.

I grabbed Bubba's phone and video called Jeff so Mom could see him. As soon as he answered, Mom's eyes opened. Jeff started by saying, "I am on my way home, Momma. You know I love you. You have been the best Momma, and I want you to know that I am trying to get home as fast as I can."

I had to bow my head because a flood of tears came rolling down my face as he continued talking.

When he was done, all Mom said was, "Be careful. I love you too." I had no doubt she was going to fight just as hard to see him again.

Noreen made it to the hospital around 5:00 or 5:30 PM that evening. She gently rubbed Mom on the arm to arouse her, so she would know she was there. Noreen told her she loved her. Mom opened her eyes for a minute but then, closed them right back.

They had already started pain meds, so she was finally beginning to get some relief. Noreen sat down, and we chatted a little. I asked if she was able to get a hold of my older brother, Vernon. She said he was down in Brownsville working.

I can't even remember if she said she did or didn't talk to him. That day was a blur. I just decided I'd video call him the next day so he could see Mom.

Shortly after Noreen got there, my oldest son and his family came in the room. Noreen awakened Mom to let her know they were there. Mom had grown quite fond of my three boys in the last year. Again, they were boys, and Mom was particular to males.

What happened next is a memory my oldest granddaughter, Briley, will never forget. A gift that was given in love and spirit.

My mom opened her eyes and raised her head up, looked straight at Briley and said, "What a beautiful little girl!"

Then she closed her eyes, laid her head back down, and drifted off back to sleep. That was the most energy she had shown since I had been there that day.

I will never forget the look on Briley's, or my daughter-in-law Hope's, face. Briley looked like she was about to cry. My son just smiled. Noreen said, "Aww, how sweet! And you *are* beautiful, Briley."

Briley was always a super sensitive child, so even she could see that her Grandma Betty was really sick this time. The door opened, and my second to oldest son, Jake, and his girlfriend, Kylie, came in.

Now, Jeff and Jake were two peas in a pod! Patsy used to say, "Tracey may act just like you, but Jake acts just like Jeff!" They both like to pick at people and have a dry sense of humor, which only makes things funnier when they say them.

Mom opened her eyes. Jake told her that she better listen to the doctors so she could get better. She really didn't say anything but grinned a little. She was so sick that it took a great deal out of her just to talk.

Looking back at Briley, I decided we might need to take a walk. Noreen stayed in the room with Mom. As we started down the hallway, Briley wrapped her arms around my waist, and we just hugged each other as we walked toward the waiting room. I needed that as much as she did.

We visited for a while, and then, Noreen joined us. It was around seven in the evening now. I knew they all had to work the next day, so we said our goodbyes. I went in and sat with Mom a little while longer. She seemed to be resting good.

As I sat and watched her sleep, my mind started thinking about how fast time had flown by. *She was seventy-nine years old! When did that happen? It seemed like it was just yesterday when she was at my house with toys from garage sales for the kids.*

All of this made me face my own mortality too. It had been on my mind a lot lately. I was not that far from her age now. It was like time had closed the age gap between us. I am only twenty-four years away from her age, and the pendulum has sped up.

I now know why mom wanted her grandchildren and their children to know how important it was to have their salvation nailed down. The world we once knew is changing so rapidly but also easily tainting the thoughts of those we love so dearly.

The age group of fifteen to forty now has such different views than what was had by her generation. Living together without being married, teenagers having babies, abortion, drinking, and lastly, you don't need church. It's the new "norm" and not the exception. I see it all around, and it scares me and causes me to have sleepless nights.

God is real and so is His judgment and wrath. Men are responsible for the spiritual well-being of their families and will stand before Him to answer for it. Mothers are responsible for the teaching their children. Church is a necessity, not a burden. I haven't found anywhere in scripture that says we should just sit at home and say our nighttime prayers. Instead, I have found where it does say,

> *And let us consider how we may spur one another on toward love and good deeds, not giving up meeting together, as some are in the habit of doing, but encouraging one another—and all the more as you see the Day approaching. If we deliberately keep on sinning after we have received the knowledge of the truth, no sacrifice for sins is left, but only a fearful expectation of judgment and of raging fire that will consume the enemies of God. Anyone who rejected the law of Moses died without mercy on the testimony of two or three witnesses. How much more severely do you think someone deserves to be punished who has trampled the Son of God underfoot, who has treated as an unholy thing the blood of the covenant that sanctified them, and who has insulted the Spirit of grace? For we know him who said, "It is mine to avenge; I will repay," and again, "The Lord will judge his people." It is a dreadful thing to fall into the hands of the living God.* (Hebrews 10:24–31 NIV)

Time is the most valuable gift given to us, yet we spend it so wastefully. I began to pray to not be allowed to waste what time I had left. I prayed to be a better steward of my time.

After a brief time, Kris came in with his wife and daughter, so I left to give them some time alone. They video called Kris's son, Klay, who was in the military, so he could talk to his grandma. He told her he was going to try to get leave to come home.

Kris was my mom's first grandchild, and he has the sweetest nature about him. They had a special bond too. As life does for everyone, it got busy for all of Mom's family. None of us got to spend as much time as we would have liked with her. But I could tell Kris's heart was hurting for his grandma. He was always so sweet and gentle with her.

Bubba and I were still in the waiting room. My youngest son, Wade, called Bubba to check on Mom. He had a one-year-old and a pregnant wife at home, so a hospital was no place for either of them. We told them not to come, and that we would just keep them updated.

Tracey was calling and checking in on her. I tended to use Tracey as my medical expert. I depended heavily on her to explain things, so I was constantly sending pictures of the medicine hanging from the IV or pictures of Momma. We talked a lot and often cried a lot together.

When Kris's family finished visiting with Mom, they came down to the waiting room with us. I tried to tell them what the doctor said. Kris's wife, Heather, was a nurse too, so she understood more than I did. She didn't really say much that night, but I think she knew Mom was in a crisis now.

After everyone left, I went back to Mom's room. I just wanted to sit with her. I rubbed her head and told her I wasn't going to let her go through this alone. I said, "Momma, I love you." She never opened her eyes, but said, "I love you too."

The nurse came in and gave Mom some more pain medicine. Bubba and I stayed until about ten or eleven that night before we finally decided to go home. If I wanted to get back up there early enough to catch the doctor, I needed to go home and get to bed. I kissed Mom on the forehead and told her I would be back in the morning.

Here is the thing I did not know. Nothing about my mother's condition had been spoken aloud or verbally communicated to me. I was always just told that she had poor health, which I already knew, and that she shouldn't have surgery on her feet.

I was still outwardly operating on the assumption, not the heartfelt feelings, that my mom just needed a stiff antibiotic and some fluids.

I just wasn't going to let her go through this alone, like she did when she had her hip surgery. I wasn't going to assume the worst until I was told by a doctor straightforward that Mom was not going to get any better, even though the Lord was speaking truth to my heart, preparing me for the next day. I was just chalking that feeling up to emotions and exhaustion, but looking back, it was Him, and I knew it.

Chapter 7

Facing Reality

The next morning came, and it seemed like I had just fallen asleep as my alarm started to go off. I had a tough time winding down that night. I kept waking up and checking my phone to make sure I didn't miss a call. Bubba decided he would go to work for a little while that morning, to get some things taken care of. I, on the other hand, had already called my boss and let him know I was not coming in. I explained what was going on. I am very blessed with the Christian people I work with. He was all about family and told me not to worry about anything, to just take care of my mom, and he would be saying a prayer for us.

I was back at the hospital a little before seven that morning. When I went to the nurses' station to see how she did, they were very encouraging. They said she rested well, and her vital signs were good. *Yes! The antibiotics are kicking in!*

When I went into Mom's room, she was still asleep. I just sat in silence until a nurse came in, waking Mom up. It was funny because she looked at me and said, "Don't you ever go home?"

I just looked her in the eye and replied, "I told you I'm going to be here through all of this, and I am not leaving until I have to."

She just said, "I know you will." I couldn't tell if that was sarcastic or not, which tickled me a little.

I took a journal with me, along with my Bible, so I could continue doing a study I started in the book of Jeremiah. I would read a little, then write a lot. I guess the reading was hard for me to focus on, but writing gave me a way to release my feelings. I shared openly with God how I was feeling, without having to speak it out loud.

A few nurses came in and said they were going to shift her to the other side, so I stepped out. I heard Mom cry out in pain, and I just cringed. It made me feel so worthless, like I should have been in there fighting them off. When I got to go back in, I could tell she didn't want to talk. I just stroked her hair a little. She loved having her hair messed with. I said a small prayer for God to please let her rest. She looked so tired, and the smell in the room was still so unbelievably bad.

Mom opened her eyes a little while later. I asked if she needed anything else. She nodded no, and I continued reassuring her that I was there and wasn't going anywhere. She closed her eyes again and began to drift back off.

The small petite doctor I saw the night before stuck her head in the door somewhere around 11:00 AM. She quietly asked me to step into the hallway to talk. I just figured she didn't want to disturb Mom. I wasn't prepared at all for the conversation that followed.

In a very gentle tone, she started by saying, "Your mom has a lot going on. She's septic, she's having heart problems, and her wounds are just not healing. It just isn't looking good for your mother. I don't know how to say this without being honest, but I really wasn't expecting her to make it through the night."

She paused before asking, "Can I say it?"

I was not exactly sure what "it" was, but I answered, "Yes."

I was quickly followed with, "Hospice needs to be called."

That took my breath away. Had I known all of that, I would have never left that hospital that night. I felt like I was the worst person in the world at that exact moment. I was beyond overwhelmed, guilt ridden, heart punched, and just wanted to sit down. I leaned against the wall, and again, a flood of tears came.

I looked up at her and asked, "Should I be calling my family in? Are you saying she's dying?"

She gently said, "If you want her to be able to recognize them and talk to them, then yes. I can't promise anything right now. No one has a precise expiration date. Only God knows when they will go. I'm just saying she has too much going on, and the prognosis isn't good. I am so sorry to have to tell you all of this."

I was trying hard to keep my composure. She continued, "I need you to go in there and be honest with your mom. She has the right to know."

There aren't enough words in the English language to describe the amount of weight that the request she gave me carried. The hurricane of emotions that were rushing through my entire body is indescribable. How do you tell someone they're dying? I felt that, because I'd be the one telling her, it would make me responsible for it happening to begin with! My whole being was screaming with emotion and pain. Those screams had to be heard in the heavens with a deafening sting. I know because it was deafening to me! My mind was repeating over and over, *I am simply not strong enough to do this. Please don't make me do this!* Even though you know the day is coming, it will still hurt deep down when reality hits that it is here!

The doctor patted my shoulder and left me to myself. I was completely by myself, until I suddenly felt a calming presence beside me. I just stood there for a minute and let it bring me down off that cliff. Finally, I drew a deep breath and walked back into Mom's room. Surprisingly, her eyes were open, and she was laying on her right side. I sat down in the chair next to her bed. She looked at me and said, "Has something bad happened?"

I just replied, "Everyone is fine, Momma, but I need to talk to you." I was trying not to let my voice quiver, but it was no use.

I continued, "Momma, you are really sick this time. The doctors said they can't fix this."

My tears couldn't be held back any longer as I continued, "Momma, you're dying." There, it was said. I just wanted to crawl in bed with her and let *her* console *me!* How selfish is that?

Her expression never changed. She just looked at me with a look I had never seen on her face before. It was a look of complete surrender. I asked her, "Do you understand what I am saying?"

She answered without changing her expression, "I'm dying." I ducked my head down and just started weeping.

I hadn't cried like that since my brother died in 1980. I remember laying on my parents' bed, begging for God to take me instead, and bring him back. They wouldn't miss me the way they missed him.

The only difference now was that I just wanted forgiveness from my mother! I looked up and told her I was so sorry for not being the daughter I should've been. I asked her if she would forgive me for being so selfish. I told her I was so sorry for everything I ever said or done to hurt her in any way, shape, or form.

I hurt so deeply that it felt like my throat was closing. My heart was pushing up all those years of dissension, jealousy, selfishness, and self-serving guilt so it could be dealt with. No more hiding it in the shadows, as it was all coming to the surface. I believe my mother felt the sincerity of it all. She just let me talk because I was the one that needed to do the talking. I was guilty as charged.

I love the book of James and have read it many times. It does not mess around. He cuts straight to the chase. I guess I had gotten so good at hiding how I felt for so many years, that God was going to bring this out into the light, to be dealt with. I often pray that everything that is held captive by the darkness, be brought into the light, so Satan has no power over me with it. Well, it was happening!

She was trying to absorb everything I told her, and I watched as years of her feeling unappreciated, rejected, and lonely being washed away by the confessing of my transgressions against her. The Lord was working on us both that day. I believe that with all my heart because a great healing began.

> *Therefore, confess your sins to one another*
> *and pray for one another, that you may be healed.*
> (James 5:16)

My mother had probably been doing all the praying, so it was my time to confess my sins.

Realizing Mom was still very weak, I quieted down. She then closed her eyes to rest. I bowed my head in a prayer. I had a couple of requests to ask of the God who stood by me through His Holy Spirit. I prayed He would allow my mom to wake up and be able to clearly hear everyone as they said goodbye. I asked that she be able to feel the love they had for her and pled with Him to give her the ability to say goodbye as well if it were His will to take her home. I praised Him for allowing me to have this time with my mother and to confess my sins against her and ask forgiveness. I realized that not everyone gets that chance. I also knew that it was His infinite wisdom and love for me that moved this mountain that had been not only my burden, but hers as well.

I prayed for peaceful, pain-free days. I prayed for strength for me to accept whatever His will was. I prayed that He heal her body, whatever that may take. I was praying so fast that it felt like I was babbling the prayers.

Emotions aren't my strong suit. I tend to talk fast and furious, not really knowing what I want to say. I really didn't want to say the wrong thing in a prayer to a God that was faithful to answer them. I just wanted to be able to be strong enough to get through this for her!

After I was done praying and saw she was resting, I got up to go take a walk. As I walked down the hallway, I knew I had to make the calls to the family. Strangely enough, I was calmer than I expected to be.

I sent Bubba a text message telling him what the doctor said. He texted me back to say he was on his way. All I wanted was for him to be there. He was my God-given resting place, guard, and overall security blanket.

I had come to realize over the years, that God uses the people in our lives to love on us for Him. I will never understand why He loved me so much, that he gave me Bubba and all my kids.

Then came the second call, Jeff. When he answered, I told him everything the doctor said. The phone was silent as I spoke. He really didn't have many questions. I think the Lord had been speaking to his heart, preparing him. I could tell he was tired. He told me he would be in late that night and would be up there first thing in the morning. I was glad.

All I could think of was that country song by Blake Shelton, "The Baby," and I still cry when I hear it today.

I often envied how much she loved him and him, her. I watched Jeff with Mom on several occasions when we were visiting her at the same time. He was genuine in his love for her. He was gentle, and trust me, he was not the gentle type. He was a real stinker.

I would tell Bubba, "I sure hope my boys love me like that." God knows how much I loved them!

Next call was to Tracey. I needed her to know to call her mom, brother, and everyone else she could think of.

Mom had been hard on Tracey, as she was a female. That never affected Tracey's love for her grandma. She knew that Mom had her back, even if she fussed at her. Mom never told her the word *no*. Mom trusted her and knew Tracey would always do the right thing by her.

She told me on several occasions, "Tracey always does the right thing."

I just wished my mother had told Tracey these things herself. I don't think she ever felt like Mom trusted her as much as she actually did.

I made a few other calls, and I sent a text message to Patsy's daughter to let her know what the prognosis was. I didn't want this to catch anyone by surprise. Only one knew when Mom was going home, and that wasn't me.

Chapter 8

Facing Reality Part 2

I decided to go back to Mom's room. When I walked in, I was stopped in my tracks by what I was seeing! Mom was still on her right side and her body had not moved, but now, she had her left hand held in the air. It was like she was either holding someone's hand, praising God, or surrendering.

I couldn't tell you how long I stood there just watching. I didn't want to disturb whatever was happening. I probably should have stepped back out; however, I have a great addiction. I am a "God Chaser!" If God is there, I want to be there too!

After an undetermined amount of time, I stepped forward and took Mom by the hand. I just held it for a minute and rubbed it softly. I then asked, "Momma, were you holding someone's hand?" She never responded and just laid there with her eyes closed.

I had no right to ask that question. It was between her and whoever or whatever was happening. She didn't answer, and I didn't ask again. But I will tell you this, I was extremely moved by what I was allowed to witness.

I have been told all my life about stories of people passing and things that would happen. I was petrified as a child from those stories. Now, here I was with Mom, having seen God move in some of the most powerful ways after my daddy passed.

I needed to know Mom was going to be okay. One way of knowing was being allowed to witness things like this myself. This was the first of many more things that not only I, but Bubba as well, would witness in the days to follow.

I went around and sat down in front of Mom and wrote all this down in my journal. Bubba showed up a little while later, and we just sat in Mom's room. They brought her breakfast and lunch tray, but neither one had been touched. It had to have been around one in the afternoon by now.

It was quiet in the room, and then suddenly, Mom woke up. When I say she woke up, I mean she was wide awake and alert. She was talking and joking with Bubba.

We just sat there in total awe. I asked her if she wanted anything and she said, "I would love a Diet Coke. Do you think I can have one of those?"

I replied, "Momma, you can have anything you want."

My sweet husband told her, "I will be right back." Off he went to find a Diet Coke.

The first thing I did was video call Jeff. When Mom saw him, she said, "My baby."

He said, "Yep, I am your baby. I'm headed home. I will be there in the morning to see you, Momma."

They talked for a minute, and he ended with, "I sure love you, Momma!"

She replied with, "I love you too, Jeff." The fact she spoke his name, let him know she was well aware of who everyone was and was coherent.

While they were talking, I sent a text message to Noreen to tell her Mom was awake. She texted me back and said she had an appointment to get lashes put on but that she would be there right after.

After Mom and Jeff were done talking, I took this time to tell her how much I loved her. I told her once again how sorry I was for everything. I said, "I would not have wanted anyone else but you as my momma. I knew you were the one that always made all the tough decisions."

She looked at me in a way that I hadn't seen her do since I was a little girl and said, "Tonette, I knew you were the one taking care of me this whole time. I knew all of it, and I don't know what I would have done without you!"

How great is my God? He knew I needed to hear that more than I needed to breathe. She did know I loved her! I was not a complete disappointment as a daughter. The explosion in my heart was, again, indescribable.

Mom did not mean that no one else was doing things for her, she just meant she knew how much I called the facilities, and when there was a problem, I dealt with it. I knew, and so did she, that the others were doing things as well.

I also told Momma I would take care of everyone, and she knew I would. That was something I said several times in days to follow. All I wanted was for Mom to have peace. With her not being here, I thought she needed to be sure someone would step into her shoes.

The next person I video called was Vernon. When he answered, she said, "Looky there, it's Ole' Vernon!"

They talked a minute, and she asked when he was coming home. He replied with, "I'm not coming home, Momma. I have to work. I'm a poor boy. I got lots of bills. But I love you, Momma."

She said, "Well, I understand that."

But did she really? I didn't. I really didn't know what to think at this point. His voice cracked a few times during their conversation, so I knew that he knew she was dying. I would be lying if I said I didn't struggle with this. I could tell Momma wanted him to come home. But I also knew that she recognized how hard stuff like this was for Vernon. She was grace-filled that day and accepted things as they came, which in turn, taught me to do the same thing.

I called Patsy next. I was so excited to let her talk to Mom while she was in such good spirits. Patsy needed to know Mom was going to be all right, just like I did. So I dialed her number. When she answered, Mom said, "Hello, Patsy, how are you?"

Patsy replied with, "I am fine, Betty. It is so good to hear you, and you sound like you are feeling a little better. I have been worried about you and praying for you. I miss our phone calls, and I wanted to come see you, but I know we will see each other again someday!"

I will never forget mom's reply! She said, "Oh Patsy, the things we are going to see together!" It was as if Mom had been given a glimpse of what heaven was going to be like.

Patsy sweetly said, "I bet it will be something, all right." They ended with saying how much they loved each other. I knew how hard that call was for Patsy. I just hope she realizes that was an answered prayer. I know she was praying for a chance to say goodbye, and she got it.

Patsy later told me she had been hoping Mom would just get better and pull out of this. She realized that it was different this time, she just didn't want to have to say goodbye on the phone.

The conversation between the two also let me know that Mom didn't doubt she was heaven bound. The thought of my momma walking beside Jesus with my brother, hand in hand, as He showed her all the things there was to see, brought a smile to my face.

A smile? During such a sad time? That is how God works! I sat and wondered if people realized, if they found themselves smiling after losing a loved one, did they know that was a gift from God?

The human mind has the ability to remember like a recorder. Yes, it can hold good and bad memories. If you think about how intricately the mind was created and all it can do, how can you not see the hand of God in it? Especially when all the good memories come rushing to the forefront during such a sad time.

Every good and perfect gift is from above, coming down from the Father of the heavenly lights, who does not change like shifting shadows. (James 1:17)

I was with my dad when he passed away. It was nothing at all like it was with my mother.

Daddy had a massive heart attack in August of 1996. He was sitting at the table, doing a breathing treatment, and just fell over onto the floor. Jeff was there and walked by about that same time and ran back to him. He called 911, and they had him start doing CPR. He did that until the paramedics arrived.

I was a stay-at-home mom at that time. Jeff called me, and I met them at the hospital. He was so upset when I got there that day, so I just hugged him and told him it was going to be okay. But it wasn't okay.

Daddy was put on life support, and we finally had to make the decision to take him off. He was never responsive after arriving at the hospital. Daddy was seventy-seven years old, and I was thirty.

I thought about how Jeff had to do the CPR on him that day and how hard that must have been on him. That is a big burden. I always felt bad that he had been the one to have to do it. But God knows who can and who cannot handle things, and only He knows who and why they are chosen.

After they turned off the machine, Dad started breathing on his own. It was then that they put him into a private room. I cried many tears, but I knew he was scared, and I wasn't going to leave him either.

It started to get late that night, so Noreen, Vernon, and Jeff went to rest in the waiting room and fell asleep. I sat by his bed until approximately 2:30 AM. I was so tired and was having a hard time keeping my eyes open. So I decided to lay on the other bed in his room to rest for about thirty minutes.

Bubba was with me the whole time. I asked him to wake me up after thirty minutes. I fell asleep immediately. Bubba was sitting by Daddy's bed when I laid down.

The next thing I remember was Bubba gently tapping me on the leg. When I woke up, he said, "Your daddy has quit breathing, Tonette."

I jumped out of that bed, wanting to panic, but there was an indescribable peace in the room that just wouldn't allow me to. I kissed him on the forehead and told him, "I love you, Daddy."

I walked out of the door and into the waiting room, not even turning the light on. I just looked at everyone and said, "It's over. Daddy has passed away."

They all jumped up and ran to his room. One by one, they told him they loved him, and my brothers went home. Noreen and I stayed until the funeral home came to get him.

Later, Bubba told me what happened after I went to sleep. He said he looked at the clock and it was about 2:35 AM, and he bowed his head to pray. When he realized he had fallen asleep praying, he looked up at the clock again and saw it was only 2:40 AM. That's when he immediately looked at Daddy and realized he had passed.

I will always believe that Daddy wasn't going to leave us until I wasn't watching. He waited until I didn't have to see him stop breathing. He knew how upset I had been that night. It was before my faith was as strong as it is today. But those with even the strongest faith, suffer from the pain of losing a loved one.

But I never got to say everything I wanted to say to him before he was unresponsive. Yes, he could probably hear me, but I was filled with regret that I couldn't see him looking at me when I told him how much I loved him.

Chapter 9

Life Continues Outside of the "Goodbye"

I video called my nephew, Brian, so he could talk to Mom for a bit. I could tell he was getting emotional, so I told Mom he needed to get back to work. Before I could disconnect the call, I could hear him sobbing as he set his phone in his seat.

Little did I know what he was going through with a friend of his, and the toll it was taking on him. I also knew that his maternal grandmother was someone of great importance to him. Losing her was devastating. I didn't want to cause him any pain, but I also knew how much finding him meant to Momma, and he felt the same about her. He was her grandson that continued the family in my brother's place, the brother I lost in 1980. We didn't find Brian until he was twenty-nine. She always said she wished we had found him sooner.

Life was continuing outside of that hospital room for everyone, inside and outside of our family. Struggles, victories, work…it was all still happening, yet I was blinded by time and how precious it had become.

At this point, everyone was now aware of what was happening with Mom. She was still tired, so I let her rest. I knew Tracey and the kids were coming up there and that Mom would do her best to be lively for them.

At 1:09 PM, Bubba received a text message from Wade. I heard his phone go off. I asked, "Who is that?"

To which he replied, "Wade. He's trying to play a prank on us."

The text message said, "Don't show Mom!" And included a picture of an Xray. He showed me the Xray, then quickly realized it wasn't a prank. He said, "That *is* Wade's leg! There are the screws from when he was ten and broke his ankle!"

We quickly stepped into the hallway, and I asked, "What happened?"

A new panic set in. I was thinking to myself, *This can't be happening.*

Bubba tried to call him, but it went to voice mail. I called Tamra and asked her if he was just messing with us or if his leg was actually broken.

To shorten the story, Wade did break his leg. Tamra finally got to him, and I was on overload! I was super worried about him because he had compartment syndrome when he had a broken bone last time, and this break was severe!

I realize he is a grown man. But men do not think straight, and Tamra was not fully aware of all of this and already had a lot on her plate. So I did what most mothers would do. I called that orthopedic doctor's office and told them about his history. This was a dangerous condition, and they needed to watch it closely. This break was severe, so it only increased the danger.

To say the least, I was red lining in the stress department at this point.

Once I knew that Tamra was with Wade, and Able, our one-year-old grandson, was with Hope, I pushed that to the side to deal with the crisis at hand.

The reason I know God answers prayers is because the women I prayed for God to bring into my boys' life. He was faithful to do so. My boys married women of strength! I couldn't have been any prouder of my family during this time.

Jake and Kylie brought food to Wade and Tamra, as well as Dustin and Hope. They all knew I had my hands full, and all stepped up to take care of their little brother and his family! If Wade or Tamra needed something, they were Johnny on the spot!

That is a family to be proud of, and once again, I knew I had done nothing to deserve them. They were an undeserved gift!

It was a Friday, and the day just flew by. I guess everything with Wade made it pass quickly. I was in and out of Mom's room.

At somewhere around 3:00 PM, Noreen and John, her boy-friend, came up to visit with Mom for a little while. Bubba and I always tried to excuse ourselves from being in Mom's room when people came to visit to give them time alone.

I think this was the first time Mom was meeting John, and that was Noreen's time. I wanted them to have all the time they needed with each other. Not only so Mom could see how John was with Noreen but how happy he made her.

Mom needed to know that Noreen was going to be taken care of. She worried a lot about Noreen, and knowing she would be leaving her soon, this eased mom's mind.

After they left that day, I went back to her room. She told me to be happy for Noreen and make sure Tracey and Kris were too. She went on to say she liked the way John treated Noreen and that he would take care of her. That put Mom at peace, and I was grateful for that.

They had to leave shortly after their visit to run some errands.

Tracey, her husband, Daniel, and her three boys, Christian, Colten, and Camden; came in around five or five thirty that evening. Mom lit up like a Christmas tree! She was so glad to see every one of them.

Tracey showed pictures of times passed, and they had a really good visit. Mom told each one how proud she was of them. This was the best time she had so far that day. She waited patiently for them to show up and they did! It was the lottery for her, and they got to visit for a good while.

Mom got tired, and they knew that others were coming to see her, so they came to the waiting room to visit with us.

Kris and his family, Heather, Lillie, and her boyfriend walked in. They went back to visit. Another enjoyable time for her.

The elevator opened again and in walked Zack, Vernon's son, and Kelli, Zack's mom, who was still very much a part of the family. Zack was still recuperating from hip surgery and was still using a walker. But it was so good to see him and Kelli!

They said all their hellos to Tracey and her family. Tracey had to leave because it was getting late and little Camden had not been feeling well, so we said our goodbyes.

I walked Zach and Kelli back to Mom's room. I knew Mom would be ecstatic to see them both, and sure enough, she was.

I watched as Zach just kissed and loved all over Mom. He did it like she was a little kid, and he was stealing all her sugars. I fought tears back as long as I could because it brought such a warmth to my heart to see the both of them together. Kelli loved all over Mom as well. I know that she always held a special place in her heart for Kelli. Mom still considered her one of her own.

By this time, Mom was energized by the joy that this day held from all of visitors. It was like her birthday surprise all over again.

I saw how the room was filling up, so Bubba and I went for yet another walk. I knew Mom had her heart full of love at that moment, and I wanted everyone to love on her while they could.

Kris and the rest of his family all came to the waiting room. That Lillie had me rolling in laughter, telling stories about Mom. She said that the first thing she did when she went into see Mom was to say, "Look Grandma, I have a boyfriend! I won't die old and lonely with just my dogs after all."

I looked at her and said, "What?"

She said that when Mom saw her graduation pictures, she said to Lillie, "Oh Lillie, you are going to die an old maid with just your dogs."

I just started laughing! That was exactly what I would have expected out of Mom. She always just said what was on her mind.

Lillie told another story of how every time she got in Grandma's car, Grandma would say, "You see that there?" There would be a belt laying in the floorboard.

Lillie would say, "Yes, Grandma, I promise I will be good."

What made that story even funnier is that Lillie was this sweet, passive little girl. We all knew that belt was there for Klay, not Lillie. Mom was just trying to get her bluff in on Lillie, just in case.

Klay was a pistol when he was little, and I believe he broke Mom before she broke him. It was hilarious to see those two together. He could infuriate Mom faster than any other kid in the family. And if I was honest, I think she found that more amusing than frustrating.

He always outsmarted her! He was, and still is, the sharpest knife in the drawer.

Kris told of one time when Mom was watching the kids for him. Klay refused to mind Mom. No matter what she said, he just would not do it. That boy was strong-willed! She chased him all over their house trying to spank him. He had a cast on his arm, and she finally caught him in the bathtub, where he jumped in to get away.

She was doing her best to still spank him as he held his cast out of the way, and he was just laughing the whole time.

She just kept yelling, "Stop that laughing!" Knowing Mom, she got tired before he did.

Her nickname for him was "that little stinker!" But just like all her great-grandkids, they had a special bond. One they would later share forever.

It's ironic, how a time that we were all saying our goodbyes was filled with so much laughter. She enjoyed all the stories as well. Zach and Kelli came out from their visit. Since it was getting to be 7:00 or 8:00 PM, they all decided to go grab a bite to eat.

Bubba and I sat there for a minute, just letting the events of the day sink in. We talked about the valleys and how life just seemed to cave in at times. As we revisited all the stories told, we laughed again.

Then, silence set in. Reality wasn't going to let go of us. This was one of those seasons in life that you just don't ever look forward to. But *"to everything there is a season, a time for every purpose under heaven."* That is where our faith came into play. We had both been here before so many times in the last few years. Again, I don't know how people face life without the promises of God!

We went back to sit with Mom for a little bit. She was exhausted by now. I told the nurse it was time for some more pain medicine, hoping it would help her rest.

I could tell she was finally relaxing. I knew I wanted to get back up there early again the next morning, and it was already after 9:00 PM. Jeff was coming in, and I wanted to be sure I was there. I didn't know how Mom would be doing, and it was hard enough knowing what wounds she was dealing with for him.

Chapter 10

Baby Comes Home

Bubba and I got back to the hospital about 7:30 the next morning. I checked in with the nurses, and they said she was a little restless the night before.

Until now, her medicine was morphine. That tended to make me agitated when I had to take it, so I wondered if it was doing the same thing to her. I made a note to ask the doctor for a different pain medication.

I went into the room. Now that she was awake, we talked a little. I asked if she was afraid, her reply was, "I'm not afraid to die. I'm afraid of what will happen when I die."

I asked, "Are you afraid of what will happen to your kids and grandkids?"

She didn't really answer, but I continued. "Mom, you know I will do what I can to take care of things. Please don't let that be something you fear. We are all adults now with our own families. You never really were in control anyway, and you know that."

She just said, "I know. I've been very fortunate with my family, and I know it."

I think what she was saying was that even though we all had our issues, they weren't as bad as they seemed sometimes.

I finally asked, "Mom, is there anyone special that I need to give your mother's ring or that Seiko watch to?"

She looked at me and said, "You'll know who to give it to when the time comes."

I didn't understand that answer at all. I just figured she had told Jeff or it was written down somewhere. But if I had known how profound that thought was, I would not have believed it.

Mom looked like she had a lot running through her mind on this day. Not sure what her thoughts were, I just knew they ran deep. Mom had seen just about everyone at that point. And those she hadn't seen would be there soon. We were waiting on Klay and his wife to get there, but I knew it would be late that night before they came in.

Jeff and Tina got there about ten that morning. I could see relief on his face when he came in and Mom was awake. She was on her second Diet Coke. She had also drunk a little bit of a Butter Pecan Boost, so she had a little energy. I thought both Mom and Jeff were going to cry but neither did. However, there was a tenderness that was so obvious between the two. She knew his heart was hurting, and he knew she wasn't wanting to say the word *goodbye,* so they just visited.

I left the room for a little while and then, went back in. Jeff left to get a drink, and Tina stayed behind with me.

She was moving Mom's pillows around. I was allowed to witness yet another moment I will never forget.

Mom looked at Tina and said, "Tina, thank you for letting me be a grandmother to your kids. They mean a lot to me, and I thank you."

As I looked at Tina, her eyes welled up with tears, even though she claimed later they didn't.

As she tried to busy herself to keep from crying, she softly said back to Mom, "Betty, they love you, and you have always been good to them."

Mom just seemed to keep looking at Tina as if she were trying to remember every aspect of her face.

Jeff came back in, and Tina went to go sit in the waiting room where Bubba was. Jeff and I visited a little as Mom dozed in and out. I told him about what happened with Tina and Mom. He just sat quietly.

The doctor stuck her head in the door, so we stepped out. I was so glad it finally wasn't just me talking to the doctor.

She started by saying she was going to have to discharge Mom. She said that keeping her there on antibiotics was only going to complicate things. Mom just simply did not look to be pulling out of this. She was very weak, and the doctor thought it was time to get Mom somewhere to keep her comfortable. She went on to say that she would check on a few places, along with the facility she was currently in, and get back to us. As she left, Jeff went back to the waiting room where he found Tina reading a book.

My main concern was about family being able to come and go without COVID restrictions.

Nurses came in to do wound care, so I went to the waiting room as well.

The first thing Jeff said was, "I asked Tina about what you said, and she doesn't know what you are talking about."

I just laughed and replied, "Say what you will, but I saw it. You ain't as tough as you want to be."

She continued denying it ever happened. Bubba and I both laughed. She was a softy and just didn't want people to know.

After I thought they were done with the wound care, I went back in, and Mom was on her right side again. They told me they had just given her pain meds, and Mom looked like she was sleeping.

Jeff came back in a minute or two later and sat on the other side of the room. We had a conversation that I think upset Mom. She was cringing and ducking her head down. It almost looked like she was praying. I couldn't really tell what was going on with her at that moment. I told Jeff to take a walk, so he did. I knew watching her like this bothered him.

I just started talking to Mom. I said "Momma, you know everything is going to be done the way you want it. I will make sure that we take care of each other." Then, I prayed, and she quieted down.

As a mother, I know how the heart is pained when one of your children is hurting, angry with another, or simply just exhausted. All a mother wants for her children is for them to be happy and at peace with themselves and each other.

God was so loud that day when He spoke to my heart. He just kept running scenarios through my mind, and how certain times made me feel as a parent, because that is how He felt about us and our actions. I couldn't believe how humbling this whole time was. He is still speaking today. It was a time of bringing me, yet again, to a realization of my need for humility.

It is no different than what God wants for us either. Our country has been at war with itself for years now, and we are entering into a new season. Everyone is anxious, angry, or overwhelmed with how to make a good decision. Some choices are simple ones, but others could have great repercussions down the road.

Whatever it is, God's word is here for us to make those decisions in line with His will for our lives. His Holy Spirit guides us through the scriptures, and all we have to do is be willing to stop, look, and listen.

Since time began, we have questioned why some die and others don't. Death doesn't ask permission and neither does life. Life is a gift. Yet there are those who choose to end life voluntarily while others fight to try to keep it.

We're always going to struggle with understanding why bad things happen to good people. Yes, terrible things are happening all around us, and in the world of some, it is even worse.

But we must choose life, even in death. If we don't, then where is the hope? I would rather live my life in hope than live in the darkness of hurt and pain. I know that the pain we suffer in losing someone is not ever going to go completely away. But if we choose life, we have the hope of being with them again one day.

Hope is that eternal life I plan to share with my loved ones. That eternal life can only happen one way.

The pain I suffered at the early age of thirteen, losing my brother, was so intense that I didn't think I would ever recover from it. My mother lived in the darkness for a season afterward. Even then, God was loving on me and easing my mind. He allowed dreams of comfort. He gave me gifts to do things not everyone else could.

Does it still hurt today? Yes. But my hope lies in that of Jesus Christ. I will be with Him, my brother, father, and now, mother someday. There was no doubt what I was experiencing was meant for me.

Jeff and Tina came back in a short while later, and Mom was now asleep. They said they would be back and were going to try to bring Liz and the baby when they could. I just continued to sit by Mom's bedside as she rested.

At one point, I heard Mom say, "Hey."

I looked up and asked her, "You okay?"

She looked at me very gently to reply, "Are you going to be all right?"

Looking her straight in the eye, I told her, "Momma, out of all your kids, I got this. I am going to be fine."

She smiled and closed her eyes. That is all Momma really needed to know. She wanted all of us to be all right, and I think the only way was to be able to see us.

My heart was exploding with such joy and pain simultaneously! The last time I saw that kind of concern on her face for me, was before my brother died. And here we were, better than we had been together in a long time. Why did it have to be during our "goodbye?"

I just sat and watched her sleep for a long while, letting my mind go back in time to so many memories I had of my childhood. It was like a video started playing. I caught myself smiling again, but the only difference with this smile was the soft tears falling.

After that day, I would go into the bathroom when I felt a meltdown coming on. Her mind needed to be at ease, and if she saw me crying, it wouldn't have been. Not all my tears were due to sadness. Somewhere in the emotions exchanged between her, me, and others, they were tears of gratefulness.

It was all about her now, and I knew what had to be done.

Mom's nurses at the hospital were exceptional. She had a few more calls and visitors that day, so overall, it was another good day. Wade was having problems with pain management, so we were a little preoccupied at times. He was due to have surgery the following Tuesday at the hospital that Mom was currently in.

I don't believe in coincidences, so many thanks were given during our prayer time. Our lives had taken many twists and turns over the last few years. I understood this to be His mercy falling on us. Life does not stop for anyone to catch up. But it sure seemed to me He slowed it down for a bit, just to allow Bubba and I to catch our breath. Because we were, indeed, a tad winded on *this* journey.

After Jeff and Tina left, the doctor came back to tell me they would be discharging Mom that day. She had worked something out with her nursing home. They were going to put Mom on palliative care. It was supposed to be just like hospice.

I asked her if we could have just one more night there. She very thoughtfully said, "I can make that happen." I know how strict hospital protocols are, and my belief is that was the hand of God and nothing less.

With all the COVID restrictions, I just wanted one more day of unlimited visits to whomever showed up.

Klay "That Little Stinker" finally made it home. It was around 7:30 or 8:00 when Kris brought the whole crew up to see Mom. It had taken a lot to get the leave arranged for him to come home. I made sure Mom knew how hard and far that Klay and his wife worked to get home to see her. She needed to know that she was special to him as well.

I had to chuckle when I thought about Mom chasing him around the house that day!

Before we left on Saturday night, I could see she was wincing her face again. Mom had been restless yet again all night, and the smell was ever present. I hated that.

It brought the thought of her feet to my mind and what horrible shape they were in. I don't know that I could've withstood the pain she was experiencing. It was during those times I prayed that God just take her home. I didn't want her to suffer anymore, and asking that of Him was hard. I had a tough time with understanding why she was having to suffer through all of this. All I could do was to stroke her hair and talk softly to her. But today, I am thankful He didn't take her all the times I asked

Chapter 11

Moving Day

As I got to Mom's room on Sunday morning, she was wide-eyed. She started asking if I had heard anything from specific people in the family that she was curious about, and I would answer as she went down the list. I guess she just wanted to see them again and love on them while she could. We would talk when she had the strength, and when she was done, she would drift back into a light sleep.

Noreen came to visit that day. Bubba and I took a walk and ended up in the corner of the waiting room afterward. She came in there with us a brief time later. We talked about what the doctor said and where Mom was going next.

I asked her how Vernon was doing with all of this. She said he didn't like coping with things of this nature. She went on to say, "I know y'all are mad about him not coming home, but that is just the way some people deal with this type of stuff."

I, in turn, replied, "Noreen, I don't believe anyone is mad. I just know that regrets are hard to deal with. We've been given a chance to say goodbye, and not everyone gets that. It is his decision, and we all know that. I just don't want this to haunt him, that's all. It's just like me. No one is asking for me to stay all this time with Mom. I don't feel like I have to, nor do I feel like all of you are expecting me to. I want to, and it is my decision."

Mom had been the best teacher at grace and mercy in the last few days, who was I to exercise anything less?

Jeff, Tina, Liz, and little Cameron showed up a short time after Noreen left. Mom was so incredibly excited to see that little feller. He is such a happy baby, which made it all that sweeter.

She loved the babies. She had two new great-grandsons and didn't really get to have much time with them due to the whole pandemic crisis. But I know they took him to see her while in rehab, and Jeff always said her whole countenance would change with him there.

I did notice how such a new life, like Cameron, would rush in a light of joy to the elderly. Anytime a little one showed up at Mom's assisted living facility, the whole place just got brighter. It was like they drew from the force of such youth.

I remember one time when we took Able to see Mom, there was a lady that wouldn't leave the door. Mom got so agitated because that was *her* great-grandson, and she didn't want that old lady stealing her smiles from him.

When we left that day, Bubba laughingly said, "I was waiting on your momma to tell that lady to get lost!"

I started laughing with him. Mom was not above saying that to someone.

Mom and I were alone, at one point, when she asked what day it was. I told her Sunday and said we were missing Sunday services. She just said, "I sure miss *my* friends at my church."

I understood that feeling. She had become quite comfortable with that little country church, and she adored all the friends she made there. I could see sadness starting to set in on her face, so I thought that playing some gospel hymns would help cheer her up.

I found the *Precious Memories* album by Alan Jackson and pulled it up on my phone. I made sure the words came with the songs, and we started singing. Mom perked up immediately. I held my phone up, so she could read along. We seemed to have drawn a crowd. I noticed a nurse at the door watching us. She was probably thinking, *"Her daughter should invest in lessons if she's going to sing in public!"* Ha-ha!

But I didn't care. Here was my mother, knowing her time was counting down and yet, she was praising God! It still gives me goose bumps when I think about it. Jeff walked in, listened for a minute, and left. I just grinned because I bet his ears were hurting from my singing as well. After about four or five songs, Mom was a little revived, so we stopped singing to let her catch her breath and stop torturing "Rotten Ole' Jeff."

To be honest, at this point, I thought Mom might just pull out of this. She didn't seem to be doing as bad as when she first arrived at the hospital. And with elderly people, you just don't know from day to day what will happen. Again, another lesson of who is in control.

She sure had a good visit with them all that day. Liz, once again, was so gentle with Mom. It was as if Liz hurt for her. Not that she was only hurting at the thought of losing her but that she actually felt Mom's heart hurting.

It's such a rare trait to find in our people today. My entire family has been very blessed with young men and women in it being of that same nature, from my sons and daughters-in-law to my nieces and nephews.

Cameron started getting a little restless, so they came to the waiting room, and I went back in with Mom.

The doctor came in to tell us that it was time to start moving her back to the nursing home. I had already talked to the administrative office there at the facility. They assured me they would have Mom in a private room, with no limits on visitors, and that they would be moving her that afternoon. I let everyone know.

I knew that Kris and his family, along with Zach and Kelli, were planning to come up to visit. I sent them all texts to meet us there. Jeff told me they were going to go grab a bite to eat and would meet us over there as well.

They finally got Mom moved, and it was well past lunch by then. When I came in, I did the usual temperature taking and filling out the questionnaire and went on back.

Bubba went to Mom's old room to retrieve her things. She had a wax warmer that softly glowed and flickered like big city lights at night. I wanted her to have it in there because it created a calming effect. She also had all the pictures we had taken up there for her. Kelli and Zach came in shortly afterward.

We were all in her room when a nurse came in. She told us that Jeff and his family was at the door, and that we already had to many people in the room. I told her of the arrangement made prior to Mom coming back, and she confirmed them. All was allowed in and stayed for a couple of hours.

Mom did not seem to tire of everyone being there. I knew where her strength was coming from, and she did too.

I sat in the corner of the room that day and just watched in total amazement at how well she did. I saw how everyone rallied around her. Jeff and Tina stood back a little too. Liz was knelt at Mom's bedside. Zach and Kelli just reminisced with her.

At one point, a unique gift was given to my mom. Zach video called his brother, Nick. Mom hadn't seen Nick since he was really young, and he was now a grown man.

I watched as Mom tried to take in every inch of that screen Nick was on. Little did I know how her heart longed to be in his and his sister's lives, or of the sacrifice she made. She didn't want to ever cause grief due to her desire to be with them. I knew this because when we had to move Mom's things from her assisted living, she had a little wooden box that said, "Grandma's Treasures."

In this box were several things of sentiment. One item was a handwritten note from a five and six-year-old Nick and Katie. It said something like, "Thank you for all the Christmas gifts, Grandma. I love you." They both wrote in it. Mom had that note for over twenty years now, and to her, it was her connection to them—a nugget of gold.

He told Mom he loved her, and I could tell by the look in her eyes that she knew he was sincere in that proclamation. He even got to tell Mom a secret that she was just thrilled about knowing. I think in some small way, it made Nick feel good to be able to bring some joy to a dying grandmother that he knew loved him, even if he didn't have the chance to grow up around her.

Again, I stand on how blessed we are with the young people in my entire family. This says so much about the matriarch of such a family. God was removing so many scales from my eyes, and I prayed He was from others as well. Mom did good in this life He had given her, and we had so much to be thankful for. Yes, there were many bumps and falls, but where we were standing now, roared of how He used her to instill a good foundation. What a legacy!

She was so upbeat and energetic that day. Still, in my heart I began to feel a shifting. I knew that this was that last push of strength they say happens in the end. I firmed up my conviction that day to not let her go through this alone.

Kris and his family came in about two or three hours later. Cameron was beginning to get tired of being locked in such a small space with so many people. At one point, we had twelve people in that room.

Jeff and his crew left shortly after Kris and his bunch got there. Zach and Kelli were the next to follow, which gave Mom more time with Klay and his sweet little wife before they had to return back to their Colorado base.

It was coming up on 8:00 PM now, and everyone could tell Mom was getting really tired. The last of the visitors had left, but I was not ready to go just yet. I was setting up her night light while nurses came in to give her pain medicine. It had been a long day. It was just Mom, Bubba, and me in the room. I moved all the stuff Bubba brought from her room out of the way, and Mom seemed to be settling down to rest.

I then noticed that Mom started wincing and curling up like she did the day in her room when Jeff and I had been talking. She would get real tense and then curl up. Then, she would relax a little bit. As I watched, I noticed she would jump just a little and then wince and curl up again.

All of a sudden, it hit me. The medicine was slowing her heart down, and her defibrillator was firing off. I took a video of it to send to Jeff and Tracey and see what they thought.

The nurse came in and gave her something else. I'm not sure what it was, but it seemed to make Mom relax and stop tensing up. When I saw that it stopped completely, I decided it was time for us to go.

Chapter 12

Hospice Comes In

Monday morning, I got up with Bubba. As he was getting ready for work, I was packing my bag to go back to Mom's room. I took a small speaker up there to play soft music for Mom, thinking it might help to relax her. We left at the same time.

When I got there, Mom was still asleep, so I just sat down to write in my journal. I wrote a lot during this time. Some of it just prayers, other was thoughts or the day's events. It helped to keep me centered, especially when I was writing down my prayers.

Jeff had to go back out on the road, even though I knew he was nervous about leaving. It was just me that day. I did video call him so she could talk to him over the next few days, and he always made sure she knew he would be back. It was almost as if he didn't want her to leave us just yet.

I called and let Mom talk to Tracey as well. She was working that week, along with everyone else. I knew how hard it was for her to get time off from work, and to be honest, I liked my time alone with Mom.

Mom drank her meal supplement, which was very encouraging. A couple of people that worked there came into her room that day to check on her. They heard about her condition.

One in particular was a therapist named Blair. She was a pretty and petite young lady and said she worked with Mom every time she came there.

Blair said Mom would get contrary and a little mouthy at times, but she would just give it right back to her. They developed a good relationship during that time. Mom came to really appreciate that little lady, and it was apparent that she returned the sentiment.

It was very heartwarming seeing everyone that came by to visit Mom. It was her nurses, the ladies in the administrative office, and many more.

Mom was asleep most of the day because they kept turning her over or changing the bandages on her feet. That wore her out because it hurt so bad.

Kris and his family came back that night around six. We visited for a while. The nurse came in and gave Mom her pain medications. That's when I noticed she started that tightening up again. Heather was there, and she had the same opinion as I did, that it was Mom's defibrillator. She said they should've turned it off at the hospital. She went to check the nurses' station for a magnet. She wasn't impressed with how low of a dose of pain medication they were giving her either. The fact that they didn't realize what could happen with her defibrillator was a bit concerning.

She started telling me that hospice could do so much more for Mom and that we needed to consider moving her. I just simply could not entertain moving Momma away from there again. It hurt her so badly just for them to come in and do the wound care or just roll her over. I hated it, and I was the only one having to watch it.

Klay got upset with how intense it seemed to get for Mom and left the room. After a while, they all decided to head home. I told them I would keep them posted.

But a lot of what she said made sense. I just kept brushing my hand over Mom's hair to try and relax her. Watching her tense up with such pain when no one was even touching her was heart wrenching. I stayed that night until she stopped, which was late.

Bubba called to see when I would be home. I told him what was going on and that I would go as soon as she settled down. After a while, I noticed it stopped. It was around 10:30 or 11:00 PM by then. I prayed all the way home for it to not come back.

Tuesday morning came, and when I got to Mom's room, her hair was wringing wet! I went to talk to her, but she was so exhausted that I couldn't wake her up. Mornings were usually her lively time. I was just hoping and praying that her hair being wet wasn't from sweat due to chest pains. I was hopeful that it had just been washed.

Mom didn't eat or drink that day. Her strength was beginning to fade, and my emotions were starting to bubble up again. After about two hours, she finally opened her eyes. I asked if she needed anything, and she just nodded no.

Around 9:30 AM, the administrator came in and told me they decided to bring in hospice and stop the palliative care.

Within thirty minutes, hospice was in Mom's room, evaluating her and setting up a schedule for her. We talked about Mom's pain medications. I told them she was supposed be getting Dilaudid because morphine made her agitated and informed them about the low dosage she was currently on.

The hospice supervisor, a sweet and young woman, came in to give me her card. She explained a little about what they do, and then, she prayed with me. That prayer was heartfelt and gave me a sense of relief.

I will tell you this much, I sure saw the difference for myself between hospice and palliative care. I will always recommend hospice. The change was instantaneous.

Kris later told me that Heather called Mom's facility and insisted they get hospice in there. He didn't want me to be upset that she did that. It didn't upset me at all. In fact, I was glad because I was beginning to run on fumes.

Bubba had taken off work that day because that was the day of Wade's first surgery on his leg. He also went to make sure Tamra didn't need any help to get him in and out of the car. The doctors had already prepared Tamra for the possibility of two surgeries. This one could last up to six hours, if everything went well. They arrived at the hospital around 9:00 AM. They finally took him back at around noon or so.

I walked over there from Mom's place. Hospice was still with her, so I knew she was in safe hands. I just wanted Wade to know I was there, and I knew Tamra was exhausted. I walked down and grabbed a sandwich from the cafeteria while we waited.

Able was with Tamra's parents that day, so she didn't have to worry about both him and Wade. At one point, I heard her giggling, so I looked over at her. She was watching a video that her dad sent her of him and Able. She showed it to me. It was so sweet. He was feeding Able some Vienna weenies (or so us Texans call them), and Able was loving it. Tamra lit up with such love watching that video. Every time she watched it, she got tickled all over again. It made me feel good to see her giggling. Her parents are sweet people, and she loves them so.

Wade was only back there for a little over an hour when the patient board said he was in recovery. That sparked concern. They came out and said two people could go back to see him. I told Bubba to go with Tamra, and I headed back to Mom's room. I'm sure I wore

Bubba out with text messages, wanting to know what the deal was with Wade, but I was really concerned about him and Tamra.

Apparently, the swelling was too bad to do all that had to be done, so the second surgery had to be scheduled after they got the swelling down. They were concerned about compartment syndrome.

Bubba followed them back home to make sure she got him in the house and set up. Wade is a big ole' boy, and Tamra didn't need to try handling him, being pregnant. We were in the same exact situation before and knew what a challenge that could be.

When I got back to Mom, I saw that she was awake. She visited with me a little. I told her Wade was done with his surgery but that he would be needing another one.

I just held her hand and asked if she needed anything. She said, "Not right now."

Mom liked for us to hold her hand and stroke her hair. I often wondered if she wished we were this caring when she was in good shape.

Mom was having a difficult day that day, and I could tell. She was in and out of rest. I held her hand most of the time that day and just talked about anything that came to mind. I did finally tell her about what had been going on with Bubba and I over the last few years.

She was asleep when I was telling her all of this, but I just needed to get it all out. I looked at her and would often tell her, "Momma, if God allows, come to me in my dreams."

I don't think people ever look back once they rest in the arms of God, but I had dreams after my brother and father died. They were very vivid dreams and always gave me comfort after waking up. I still remember them today.

Chapter 13

The Visitor

Once Bubba got Wade home and saw that all was well, he came back to stay a bit with me. It was about dusk, and the room had a soft glow to it from her wax warmer light. Music was very softly playing in the background, and Mom had dozed off. Bubba was on one side of the bed, and I was on the other. What happened next made us both just sit in silence and watch.

Mom opened her eyes as if someone had called her name. She was looking to her left. Her eyes followed something or someone across in front of her bed to the right side of the room. It seemed to stop there, and we watched as she raised her head a little and squinted a bit, as if she were trying to make sure that what she was seeing was really there. She then laid her head back, and her eyes went to the foot of her bed. She was literally looking into thin air. Or was it that we just could not see what she was seeing?

I looked at Bubba, and he glanced back at me. We were both just looking at Mom, then around the room, then back at Mom. I finally mouthed the words, "She sees something," to him. He looked at me and mouthed back, "She sure does."

I don't know if this only took a few seconds or if it lasted minutes. When I asked Bubba later, he didn't really know either. All I know is that it was never scary. It was the most curious yet calming presence either of us have ever experienced. We just sat in total amazement.

I finally broke the silence and said, "Mom, what do you see?"

She wouldn't answer. She just watched as whatever it was moved to the left again. After a few seconds, she closed her eyes and drifted back to sleep.

Neither of us believe it was a hallucination. We both saw his mother have one of those, and this wasn't what that looked like. He stayed a little longer, and then, he headed home.

Shortly after he left, she started tightening up again, so I called the number they gave me for hospice. I told them I thought it was her defibrillator. I had to consent to have them turn it off, a decision that was not hard to make. I thought it would have been, but I knew where she was headed. It was about 8:45 PM, and her nurse made a few calls to find a magnet. He called back and said someone was on their way with one.

I just sat holding Mom's hand, singing softly along with the old hymns playing on my little speaker I brought previously and stroked her hair. Mom never spoke a word, but I kept thinking I could almost hear what she was saying with each episode. It was a little strange, but I just chalked it up to emotions.

Within thirty or forty minutes, in walked a hospice nurse. She made the comment, "I love that smell, and this room is so soothing with the soft light. It feels very calm in here."

We chatted a little while she unwrapped this big round magnet, and she moved it around on the left side of Mom, until we heard it find and stick to the metal in her chest. She then taped it in place and left.

Mom never had another episode of the wincing with pain again. She fell fast asleep, and I could tell it was the deepest sleep since the hospital.

Looking back, I'm unsure how many times that thing went off. We just didn't know it, and she didn't know what was happening to be able to tell us. I just was sitting there, thanking God. While I still didn't understand why she had to linger in pain, I prayed for the strength to be able to accept His will for this situation.

I sat with Mom a little longer, just watching the soft twinkling of her light and taking in the words of the old hymns. They had such a deeper meaning than most people ever stop to think about. We just get so used to singing them on Sundays, that we don't slow down long enough to realize what we are singing or why.

Out of nowhere, a calm came over me that is unexplainable. The only words I would have to explain it would be,

> *Do not be anxious about anything, but in everything by prayer and supplication with thanksgiving let your requests be made known to God. And the peace of God that surpasses all understanding, will guard your hearts and your minds in Christ Jesus.* (Philippians 4:7)

I left right after that. I drove in complete silence, not wanting this calmness to end. It was like the sweetest nectar I had ever been allowed to drink.

The silence was broken briefly by my phone ringing. It was Bubba just checking to see when I would be leaving. I told him I was on my way home, and we hung up. I went back to my blissful calm state.

When I finally arrived home, I took my shower and laid down before Bubba even came to bed. I slept better than I had slept since January 20. I was still asleep when he left that next morning. He later told me that he could tell I was in a deep, restful sleep all night because I never moved. He said I was so twisted in the bed and left little to no room for him. He finally just put his legs over mine and went to sleep, and the next morning, I was still in the exact same position.

After that day, something else that amazed me began to happen. Most people will say it was all emotion I was experiencing, trying their best to explain away the Spirit of God. But for those who have had even a small taste of what was about to happen, they will stand in testimony as to the validity of it. Even if they don't, it will never change the facts. It did happen.

Wednesday, June 2, 2021. Bubba took off work that day to go with me, and while I really appreciated it, I was still really concerned about Wade and Tamra. I would've just felt better if he was there with them, in case they needed something. In addition to that, I just wanted to spend some time with Mom. The night before was filled with the presence of the Holy Spirit that I just wanted to be with Mom and share it with her. He understood it.

He just lost his mother a few years before, and he loved his little momma with all his heart, so he understood how hard a time like this was.

It was about a thirty-minute drive, and I could feel all the emotions coming on. I turned my radio up as loud as I could stand it, sang with it for about ten minutes or so, then turned it down. I started praying aloud. The longer I drove, the louder I seemed to get. I was giving unconditional thanks and rebuking the darkness I felt setting in.

If anyone had pulled up beside me, they would've thought I was crazy. I was practically yelling by the time I got on the bridge, just a few miles from where Momma was. I was not going to allow the gift we were being given to be stolen by the deceiver. God had a plan behind all of this, and I was going to trust Him.

Mom was going to be with Him for eternity, so these last few days would soon pass like a vapor, the way our lives do (*James 4:14*). If she could hang in there so could I, with the strength He had already been pushing through me.

Mom was wide awake when I got there. She was still getting weak, and I could tell with each passing day that we weren't going to have her much longer.

I told Momma, "I sure love you."

She replied, "I love you too, Tonette." I loved it when she said my name after "I love you." It made me feel like she was speaking to my very soul, and it wasn't just empty words thrown in the air.

At this point, the days were really quiet in the room, and I think that helped her some. I was using a new scent in the wax warmer since I turned it back on. It was called "Newborn Nursery," so the room was filled with the smell of babies. That was what the hospice nurse smelled the night before. We both loved that smell. What woman doesn't? To me, it was a very calming scent.

The hospice aid came in to give her a bath. I watched with such awe as she went about getting Mom ready for the day. She was the sweetest, most caring woman I had ever seen. She just talked to Mom the entire time, telling her how pretty her hair was. She was quick about her job and was more than thorough. She really did enjoy loving on her patients. Gifted was not strong enough of a word for her.

I remember thinking, *"I wish I had her compassion and ability to love unconditionally on total strangers. She must have crowns stacking up in heaven by the truckload!"*

Mom didn't seem to be hurting as bad anymore. They were very conscientious about giving her pain medicine before they did anything to move her. That was such a relief, not only to Mom but to my heart that ached for her as well.

Bubba and I texted and talked often that day. He ended up coming up there, and we went to lunch.

I knew Jeff and Tina had a lot going on as well, behind the scenes. They are very private people and keep a lot to themselves. Bubba and I used to do the same thing and to some extent, still do. However, my oldest son said something to Bubba one time that gave us a lesson in why that is not always best.

One of us had some medical issues that we had not discussed with any of our family. When we finally decided we would tell them, he told Bubba, "Why didn't you tell us about this? How can we pray for you if we don't know you need the prayer? You both talk about how powerful prayer is, so you should give us the opportunity to pray for you!"

Ouch! That stung! Sometimes, we, as parents, forget to practice what we preach. This was one of those times.

I received a text from Noreen asking if Mom needed anything. She was going to come up and relieve me. I wasn't going anywhere, but I welcomed the company. She arrived around 2:00 PM that day. Mom woke up for a minute and visited with her. She was always glad to see Noreen. She was very tired and was in and out a lot that day.

Noreen was on the left side of Mom's bed. Before Mom dozed off, she told her that Vernon would be up there tomorrow to see her. Mom said, "Good, I want to see him."

Then, she fell asleep again.

Noreen looked at me and said, "Vernon called me this morning and said he would be in late tonight. He said that something just wouldn't let him sleep last night. He said he needed to come see Mom."

The very first thing that popped in my head was what Bubba and I had witnessed the night before. The visitor that Mom had that we could not see. At that point, I let my mind run wild with it. I thought, *"Could that same visitor have been in Vernon's room that very night after leaving Mom? Could it have been strengthening him and preparing him to come see his mother for the final time?"*

I know God is capable of anything He chooses, so anything is possible. The scriptures is loaded with stories of messengers from God. All I knew at that very moment was that Mom had been waiting to see him, and he was now coming. I know she had been praying for that.

Like I said before, Mom needed to see everyone, just to make sure they were going to be okay.

After Noreen left that day, I just sat and held Momma's hand. I watched her as she slept. There were times that I could actually feel her heart speaking to mine. It had to be. There is no way I would've produce the things I could've known or wrote on my own.

That happened increasingly over the next few days. I loved every moment that was shared and every minute she was awake, looking at me. We spoke to each other yet never audibly said a word.

Later that night, Gus, Jeff and Tina's son, and his girlfriend came up to see Momma. She didn't really wake up much, but she did acknowledge he was there. He looked so sad as he watched her sleep. We talked about everything, and he asked about what all had happened but even as we talked, his eyes would turn back to Mom.

Momma loved Gus. He used to stay with her after school sometimes. I think it was more to keep her company than anything. But they formed quite a bond. He is a sweet boy and has a big heart.

She used to tell me that whoever gets him as a husband will be one lucky lady. He sure loves his momma, and that says a lot about a man. Could that be because "her boys" loved *their* momma. We all know they hung the moon, just like mine do!

Now, I know why Momma thanked Tina that day. She meant it sincerely. Being a grandmother and a great-grandmother was something Mom saw as a privileged badge of honor. She loved each one in her own way, and they loved her.

Chapter 14

The Dove

June 3, 2021, came rushing in. I arrived really early that day. I wanted to be there when Vernon got there. I know he is an early riser, but I figured Noreen was coming with him, and she is like me, not a morning person. I had to laugh a little at that. I know how I drag my feet in the mornings, and I know how impatient the men in our family are.

When I got there, I stopped at the nurses' station to check to see how she did. They said her vitals were good but that she didn't make a peep all night.

As I went in her room, I was quiet, so I wouldn't wake her. She opened her eyes a little and started mumbling something. I couldn't understand what she was saying, I was getting frustrated with myself. I sent Bubba a text and told him how I felt so helpless with that.

I told Mom, "I am so sorry, Momma. I can't understand you." She would try and repeat it. I just said, "Rest, Mom, and we will talk later."

Finally, I understood what she was saying. She was asking if Vernon was still coming. I told her as far as I knew he was, and she settled down.

Shortly around 10:00 AM, Noreen and Vernon came into the room. Noreen gently took Mom's hand, woke her up, and said, "Momma, Vernon is here."

Momma looked at Noreen and said, "Vernon, I am so glad to see you!"

She said, "No, Momma, I am Noreen. Here is Vernon."

Vernon then took Momma's hand and said, "Here I am, your favorite child." Momma turned to look at him and grinned.

She said, "I am so glad you came." He told her how much he loved her, and she told him she loved him too.

My heart crashed to the floor. It made me so incredibly sad that she thought Noreen was Vernon. I excused myself, went to the bathroom, and melted. I wanted to wail out with emotions but that would have served no purpose. I just sat down on the toilet and steadied myself. I knew what it meant for Momma to see Vernon, and I was so grateful he came.

I was thinking that she was losing her sight at this point, and that was hard to take in. Even though I knew Mom was leaving soon, it didn't make the process any easier in times like these. I collected myself, dried my eyes, and told them I would be back. I went outside and sat for about ten minutes.

I texted Bubba and let him know I might leave a little early that night to go over to see Wade. By early, I meant 6:00 PM or so.

I went back in and visited with them for a little bit. Mom had drifted back off. Before they left, they both gave her a kiss and told her goodbye. They said they would be back super early in the morning.

They were leaving to go to Missouri on Friday morning. Our half-sister had passed away, and they were going to go to her funeral. I planned on heading to work to tie up some loose ends that were needing to be done.

I stayed with Mom the rest of the day. At one point, I laid my head on her rolling bedside table, and we just held hands as I took a little nap.

Funny thing was when I woke up, my right eye was stuck shut! I started laughing, and Mom just looked at me like I was crazy. I think she was wanting to laugh but just didn't have the strength.

I left that day and told Momma I would be back early, and she just nodded. I knew she was tired, and hospice came in to make sure everything was being done like it should. I stopped by the nurses' station and made sure for the thirtieth time they had my number. I am sure those girls were sick of me telling them my contact information.

I went to see Wade that day, and it felt good. I needed to see him and his little family. They told me everything his brothers and their wives had done for them. I could tell it made Wade feel a bit humbled, that they did all that they did.

God used little Able to show me how much He loved me. That baby was so sweet. He would go over and lay his head on his daddy's chest, as if to comfort him. Able let me, and Bubba just love all over him. We needed that lovin' more that anyone knew. We stayed and bought take out and ate with them. I could tell Wade was wearing down and Tamra was exhausted, so we finally left.

I woke up at five on Friday morning, June 4, 2021, so I could see Momma before I went to work. As usual, I stopped by the nurses' station and checked in. They told me Mom wasn't very responsive since I left the day before. They assured me her vital signs were good and that she would be fine that day, but that made me overly anxious that morning.

I went in and grabbed Mom's hand and began stroking her hair. I got to visit with her as she slept for about twenty minutes before we had to leave.

It was hard to focus that day at work. I could tell I was agitated and short on responses. I noticed my Apple watch kept flashing. My heart rate had been running really high since all this started. Bubba made me schedule a doctor's appointment that day. That only made me more anxious because it would take longer to get back to Mom.

My doctor is an exceptional person. I went and the first thing she said was, "What's going on with you? Just looking at you, I can see it all over your face."

I recapped the last few months, and she said, "Girl, if you do not learn to decompress, you're going to have a stroke. Your heart rate is too high. If it gets above 140 again, you call me immediately."

She prescribed a medicine for me to take before I went to sleep every night. She wanted me to do this for a month or so.

Finally, we were headed back to Mom's. Bubba dropped me off at the front door as he left to go pick us up some burgers. I stopped at the nurses' station, and a new group was on duty. They told me Mom had been pretty unresponsive all day, but her vital signs were good. I texted Tracey to ask if that was normal, and she responded back, saying yes.

I just sat, holding her hand, and talking to Mom. I brushed my hand through her hair. I prayed a short prayer. I kept reminding Mom that Jeff would be back in late that night to see her in the morning.

I had been talking to Jeff on and off for the last few days, giving him updates. I let him talk to Mom whenever she was awake. He was putting in some long, hard miles to get back as quickly as he could.

Bubba returned with the food. Even though Mom hadn't opened her eyes yet, I just didn't feel right eating in front of her. I closed the curtain in between the two beds, and we sat at the window to eat. I wasn't really hungry, but I was shaky so I ate.

After a few minutes of trying to force myself to eat, I put the rest in the bag. Bubba and I just sat there, looking out the window at the courtyard as he finished his burger.

All of the sudden, a white bird landed about thirty or forty feet from Mom's window. It was all by itself, no other birds around. I watched that bird as it walked a straight line to Mom's window, where we were sitting. By now, Bubba had stopped eating and was watching it too. It was very odd that it was all alone, walking straight toward us, and not afraid at all. It never wavered in its direction of the window.

Without looking at each other, I asked Bubba, "What type of bird was that?"

Still looking out the window in disbelief, he replied, "It was a white ring neck dove."

He continued, "You don't ever really see them alone. Normally if you see one, you see several, and they are usually gray."

My only reply was, "Hmm."

I sat there for a second longer, my mind running wild again. I reached over and opened the curtain. Simultaneously, Bubba and I turned to look at Momma. Her eyes were wide open, and she was staring in the direction of the window. We turned and looked at each other. Then *he* said, "Hmm."

I got up and went to her bedside. She never looked at me or changed directions of stare. I brushed through her hair again and asked her if she was okay. Still nothing, same look, same direction. I really didn't know what to make of it. My mind was still running wild with what this could've meant.

David made a plea in Psalms 55:6, *And I say, "Oh that I had wings like a dove! I would fly away and be at rest;"* He was wanting out of his situation at that time.

Mom was tired of hurting, and she was needing the rest that is given in our salvation, when the earthly body is worn out.

Was this the plea my mother was making in her heart? She saw all of her children now. Was she wanting to be at rest?

I know a lot of people that would say, "You are looking for things that are not there."

To those people, I would have to say, "I serve a God that you must not know! He is capable of anything, and *I* know that. To you, this is a simple bird. To me, it was a loving God, letting me know everything was going to be over soon, and Mom would be granted that rest."

Even though she opened her eyes, she was still unresponsive. Unresponsive to *us* anyway. For all I know, she saw her visitor again. I was sad and in awe altogether. I was hoping she could hang in there until Jeff got home. I knew he needed to see her again.

The rest of the day and into the night, I just sat beside her. I held her hand again and watched her. It was getting late, and I knew Bubba was tired, so we left around ten that night.

I took the medicine the doctor gave me, and it quickly knocked me out. I did finally rest that night, at least. But when I woke up the next morning and saw it was already 7:00 AM, I rushed to get dressed and get back to Mom. Time was growing increasingly precious.

I didn't want her to be alone any longer than she had to be. I made a promise to be with her, and I was keeping that promise.

Chapter 15

A Stranger's Hug

On Saturday morning, June 5, 2021, I woke up and felt restless. I got everything ready the night before, so all I had to do was throw on my clothes and head back to Momma.

With each passing day, I was growing more uneasy about leaving her. I know me being there wasn't going to change the time the Lord would call her home, but I didn't want her to be alone too long at a time.

I have heard godly people, whom I know have a personal relationship with the Lord, talk about times they had a brush with death. Just because we know where we are headed, doesn't mean it isn't scary. We are human, and the unknown is still frightening.

I love the Lord with all my heart, and I often think of how glorious heaven will be, but the trip to get there is still a daunting task.

I have a dear friend, who recently had open heart surgery, that I know beyond any doubt, loves the Lord. When he talks about having to stay in the hospital without his wife (due to COVID restrictions) and being all alone, he tells me how uneasy he was. Not only is the unknown scary, but it is also compounded by facing it alone.

Comfort came when his wife was by his bedside, not just for him but for her as well. He knew what could've awaited him. However, he was created with the same emotions as everyone else and being a faithful Christian does not change that. It does, however, give us the fact that He has never failed us and never will. Therefore, the fear is not as intense as it is for those with no hope. These trials only strengthen the faith muscles when we see how, once again, the Holy Spirit enters in to sit in counsel with us, *if* we allow.

These same friends had a child diagnosed with cancer at one point. A thought that is even more gut wrenching. I remember how the prayers were prayed with nothing but expectations of healing. No doubt was shown. They asked with faith and expectation, and He was just and faithful to answer that prayer.

The only way I can explain the hope we have is we are hanging off the side of a cliff that has a hundred-foot drop to a rocky bottom.

All of a sudden, there is this huge hand that is so strong and firm that reaches down to us. We decide to let go of the ledge long enough to allow that hand to grab hold of our hand and begin to lift you up.

Here is the point; you have to choose to let go, having faith. Letting go of the rocky ledge, experiencing fear, will allow the connection to happen, and you'll feel the torment of the fall begin to fade.

It takes a conscience effort on our part, along with not looking down at the possibilities, to let go and grab the hand that pulls us up. I am guilty of not putting in enough effort. I have chosen to hold fast to the ledge too many times and let the torment cause sleepless nights and anxious days.

Death is not something many people look forward to. We don't buy a ticket with a time and date on it. It isn't stamped on our foreheads, and there's no crystal ball to look into that will tell us. It can be sudden, or it can be long and painful.

The only thing we know for sure is that we meet the highest statistic in the world. Ten out of ten people will die. So what we do with the gift of time that He has given to you and I is up to us.

I gave Mom a kiss and let her know I was there. I busied myself for a minute, tidying up the room, putting a new wax cube in the warmer, and set everything up for the day.

I talked to Momma again and told her that I loved her, although I believe she felt every emotion I was experiencing. Hospice told me it was important to continue to let her know we were all good. I told her Jeff had made it in and would be up some time that day to see her.

I held her hand and just stared at it. I thought of all the things that little frail hand had done. All the diaper washing, bottle making, clothes washed, meals made, tears cleared, and PTA meetings for five kids. The mail she sorted, stacked, loaded into a vehicle, and delivered. There was an endless multitude of things not only accomplished but done out of love.

As God revealed years and years of things taken for granted by me, I felt the need to journal all my thoughts. Once again, humility was having its way with me. So much to say but words just weren't strong enough. I put my pen down and told Momma I would be back. She was still unresponsive, but that was irrelevant to me. I still heard her heart speak to me as I left, "Tonette, you're going to be okay. Take a walk and just breathe."

I went outside and sat on the bench on the front porch. I was watching people come and go, all the while thinking, *"Why did I waste so much time? How long has their loved one been here? How often do they come to see them?"*

It was just a whirlwind of thoughts.

The front door opened and out walked a woman I had seen there several times. She worked in the administrative office and had long gray hair. She was always seen with a smile and sweet.

I noticed she was walking straight toward me. As she got closer, I stood up just in case she wanted to sit down. I had my journal with me, in the event the words came to me. As she got to me, she put her hand on my shoulder. She began with, "I want you to know you are a good daughter, and your mother has to be proud of you. I've seen you here every day that I have been here, and we don't see that much."

In my mind I was screaming, *"No, I'm really not that good. I complained sometimes about having to come here, I didn't stay as long as I was able to, and I didn't let her know how much I loved her when she was able to understand it. A good daughter is not what I would use to describe me!"*

I let her continue. "Just know that your momma knows you are here, and she is incredibly lucky to have you." Hearing her say these things to me made me want to cry so bad!

She hugged me with a tight, meaningful hug. I needed that hug more than I needed the words. Not that I didn't appreciate her words, I just needed the human touch. Once again, God sent the right person for the right job at the right time. It was hard to not burst into tears. I thanked her for the kind words, and she went back into the office area. I sat back down and just enjoyed the fresh air.

With the pandemic, we have all forgotten how good a hug feels, or even just a touch on the shoulder in a time of doubt.

Shortly after she disappeared, a maroon van pulled up. To my surprise, Jeff got out of it. It was his daughter's van, and they were going to take the baby for a walk. We both walked in together.

Jeff immediately went to Mom's bedside and tenderly rubbed her head as he told her he was there. I left to take a short walk around, then went back in. I knew time was short, so I wanted him to have the privacy to say whatever he needed to say.

As I went back in the room, he was still holding her hand, just looking at her. I could tell he was tired from all the driving he had been doing. He complained of his legs cramping as he was rubbing them, so he stood up to move around and stop the cramping. He stayed for a couple of hours. Around 1:00 PM, he got the call that they were headed back to get him, so he left.

My granddaughter had her first ballet recital that night, so I was hoping he could stay while I traveled for the hour and a half drive away for the recital. But I knew he had already been driving a lot that week so he could get home, and he had other things that had to be taken care of. I hated disappointing her because she was only seven and worked hard for this.

Finally, I made a call to Kris, and he said they would all come and sit with Mom while I went to see my granddaughter dance. I felt a huge weight lift off my shoulders, knowing he was going to be there. I knew he would call me first if anything happened and if I needed to get back.

I'm so glad I didn't miss the performance. She was a living doll on that stage in her little blue tutu. As I watched her, I began to cry, thinking how much my mother would have loved that! She loved to go to the programs the kids had at school. It was the highlight of her life.

Bubba just grabbed my hand, as he knew what was going through my mind. Just watching her do her little routine made his eyes well up with tears. We have been so blessed with our babies! We have so much to be thankful for.

We left around eight that night to head home, and Kris was still with Mom. He told me to go on home, and he would make sure things were set up for the night. We arrived back to our place close to 9:30. We both went straight in, took showers, and went to bed.

Chapter 16

Going Home

At five, Sunday morning on June 6, I was awakened by something. I sat straight up in bed, with a need to just get back to Mom. I felt this overwhelming longing to tell my mom a few things. I just couldn't get ready fast enough. Bubba was going to church and planned to come up there afterward, so I left him sleeping.

I just grabbed my bag and left. I made it there by six. There weren't any nurses at the station, so I just went on back to her room. She was the way I left her the night before. I knew in my heart that on that day, it was going to be my last chance to tell Momma some things I needed to say.

I sat my stuff down, and I noticed her breathing was steady. She seemed relaxed. I pulled the chair close to her, grabbed her little hand, and began to stroke her hair.

I began with, "Momma, there are a few things I need to tell you. I think you already know, but I am going to say them anyway. I have made some promises to you in the last few days."

My eyes began to fill with tears as I continued, "I told you I would take care of everyone, but the truth is, we are all adults now, and there is no need for that. We have our own families, and you have given us what we need to be successful. Noreen has John now, Vernon has his own life, Jeff has his family, and I have my own family too," I could tell she was listening as I paused.

I swallowed hard and continued, "Momma, we are now the ones taking care of our families like you took care of us. I have my hands full with just Bubba and the kids. Noreen, Vernon, and Jeff know if they need me, I will be there. But I am letting go of the caretaker role. I took that on without anyone asking me or even knowing I felt like I had to do it. You always knew, but no one else did."

I felt a wave of relief and guilt. She was very honest in her life when she spoke to people, and she deserved no less from me. I went on, "You have to know we are all going to be fine."

I didn't want her to leave me with what I saw as a lie. I needed to be honest, not only for her but for myself as well.

I know as a mother, when I am gone, I want my boys and their families to take care of each other. I want them to treat one another with respect and love. If one is in need, I would love to know they'll rise up to help. They had with Wade, so why wouldn't they when I and their dad are gone?

I could feel my mom's heart speaking to me, causing a wave of tears. It felt like she was saying, "It's okay, Tonette, you don't always have to be the one. You take on things that aren't yours to deal with. I love you!"

There were times in Mom's final days I thought I heard her speak. Some so tender, that my heart ached with having to say good-bye. I wanted a few more months now, but how unfair would that have been for her.

You would think at my age, I would have been ready to let go of my momma. But in reality, your mother is still your momma at any age, and you are reduced to the little kid you always were to her.

We spend our lives looking forward to our next move until "good-bye" comes, and then, we examine the past under a fine microscope. We see everything, good and bad, but the good should always win out.

I told her that I just needed to tell her that before the Lord came to take her. I noticed I was squeezing her hand as I spoke, so I loosened my grip and just let her know I was going to be by her side, writing in my journal.

I pulled the little rolling tray and wrote a bit. Without even thinking about it, I kept catching myself looking out the window. I couldn't even tell you what I was thinking. I decided to walk around for a minute or two.

As I went down the hall, I could hear singing coming from the cafeteria. I was drawn by the sound. It was utterly amazing. I sat down in the little waiting area right outside the cafeteria. It was so incredibly comforting. I sang all of these songs in church before and heard them a hundred times, but this time they soothed the ache in my soul. I couldn't see that many people in there, but it sounded like a well-versed choir. It was absolutely beautiful.

I took out my phone to video record it. I wanted Bubba to hear it. I took several videos. *How could it be sounding like a thousand angels singing?* I still have the videos today, and I am still just as amazed as I was that day.

All of the old hymns have always brought a calm over me. That day, they were especially calming. I had some of the greatest singers singing these very hymns in her room on the speaker, but they were no match for the sound coming from that room. I just wanted to stay there forever.

I eventually wandered back to Mom's room and grabbed her hand again. That was something I couldn't do enough of, especially since she left the hospital. There were days that I held her hand for hours. I guess I just needed that touch.

Jeff came in the room a little before noon. I got up so he could sit by her side. I walked outside for a minute, just to stretch my legs and give them some time alone.

When I got back in the room, we small talked about things going on. After about an hour, Mom groaned a little. This was the first time she had made a noise in a few days. I noticed her breathing was a little faster than before, but I didn't say anything. I knew she must've been hurting. They told me she hadn't had anything for pain, so I asked the nurse to give her a small dose.

Jeff and I continued to visit. We just sat in silence for a brief time, then Jeff turned back to Mom.

He said, "Mom's nose is running."

I got up to get a tissue, and he stood up to let me wipe her nose a little. That is when I noticed there were tears. I said, "Jeff, she is crying."

I just grabbed her hand and said, "Momma, don't you cry for us." Jeff leaned over the other side of the bed and rubbed her hair and said, "It's okay, Momma, we're all going to be fine. It's okay." I could tell he was beginning to pace a little.

Her tears kept coming. I just told her, "Momma don't you cry for us. We are going to be fine, please don't be upset."

Jeff received a text message and quickly said, "I've got to go. Tina is here to pick me up."

He told her again, "I love you, Momma," and then left.

After he was gone, I began to talk to her softly. I said, "Momma, please don't cry for us. Your Savior and son are just one breath away.

It's okay to go to them. Let go, Momma. Run as fast as you can to them."

I noticed her breathing started to slow down. I just swallowed the huge lump in my throat and continued, "Momma, just one breath away and you will be with Jesus. You will hurt no more, and you will have joy again. No more loneliness. It's hard to see you like this, Momma. All I want is for you not to hurt anymore."

Her breathing was so slow now that it was hard to see. I began to cry, but I continued, "I love you so much, Momma. Go to them and be at peace. I will miss you terribly, but I will see you again. If God allows, come to me in my dreams."

She took one last small breath, and her tears were no more. I just sat there with tears falling, saying, "I am sorry, Momma. I am so sorry! I know you had to go." I was sorry she had to leave, I was sorry I was telling her to go, and I was sorry that I wasn't better to her in life here. I sat there a minute and then pushed the nurse's button. The nurse didn't come yet, so I got up, kissed Mom on the forehead, and told her once again that I loved her. All I wanted to do was completely lose it, but just like with Daddy, I couldn't.

I went to the hallway and waved at the nurse. She came in, saw my face, and asked, "Did she pass?"

It took all I had to say, "I think so."

She checked Mom, turned to me, and said, "I'm sorry. Yes, she is gone."

She went to get another nurse as I stood up and walked over to the window. I knew I had to tell Jeff, so I called him and said, "Jeff, Momma has passed."

He said, "I'm coming right back!"

I told him there was no need to do that but he insisted, so I didn't argue.

As I was looking out the window, I felt this urge to just let go of all the intense emotions I had been holding back. I just wanted to be held and comforted, but I was alone.

Just then, as I turned to get things picked up, Bubba was standing six inches behind me. I hadn't heard him come in. I just fell into him and let it all go! I cried harder that day than I had since this all started and didn't cry that hard again.

Apparently, after Jeff had left, my phone rang. I thought I hit the decline button on my Apple watch to silence it, but instead, I somehow answered it. It was Bubba calling, wanting to know if I wanted something to eat. He could hear me talking to Momma and knew what was happening, so he came straight there. Coincidence? No. It was God once again! He held me, loved on me, and comforted me through Bubba. Perfect timing is of God!

After twenty minutes or so, the door opened, and it was Jeff. He came straight over to me and hugged me. He started saying, "I am so sorry I left you alone. I shouldn't have left!"

I told him, "Jeff, you did nothing wrong. Momma wasn't going to leave until you weren't here to see it. You did absolutely nothing wrong." He just kept apologizing.

I knew Momma's heart, and she knew every one of her children's hearts. Jeff was her baby, and she didn't want him to be there. It was hard enough saying goodbye without having to see her go. She also knew I was keeping my promise to stay with her, whether or not she wanted me to.

Jeff gently kissed Mom on the forehead and said, "I love you," and sat down. Tina just stood beside him where she belonged.

After a moment of silence, we said a small prayer. We thanked God for relieving her pain and coming to take her home.

The staff was now coming in and were busy, so we, then, had begun to pack up Mom's things. I wasn't even thinking at this point. I was just going through the motions. It was difficult to leave, but we had to.

As I got to my car to go home, Tracey called. When I told her, she began to sob. I asked her to call and let everyone know, and she said she would. I told her I just wanted to go home.

Bubba asked me to leave my car, and we would come back and get it later, but I didn't want to do that. Oddly enough, I told him all I wanted to do was turn my phone off, go home, and pick beans with Jake. He just looked at me like I was crazy. But that is what I wanted to do.

I rolled the windows down in my Jeep and rode home in silence. I just needed to breathe.

When I got home, I went in and sat down. Jake came in and sat on the couch. Just looking at the floor, he said, "Is there anything you need me to do, Momma?"

I thought, *"Here's my chance!"*

I said, "Well, you can go home, get a hat on, and meet me in the garden."

He said, "Awe, Momma. I don't want to pick any dang beans!" I started laughing.

Bubba said, "She *did* say that all she wanted was to come home and pick beans with Jake."

I just continued laughing and said, "You don't have to, Jake. It's not a big deal."

He replied, "Great! Make me feel bad!" I laughed again.

I changed my clothes and went to the garden. After about ten minutes, Jake and Kylie both came out and started picking beans. They had me laughing so hard. She had never picked beans before, and he was making it a competition as to who picked the biggest and most, as usual. I stopped at one point and just watched them. With so much going on, here I was, once again, laughing, and it was okay to do so! God is simply good that way!

One thing I had not realized on this day was that it was Klay's birthday. This was a day him and my mother would share forever.

A day that a special life was given to this world and was now the day her life in eternity began as well. Some may see this as a bitter reminder, but Klay will hopefully see it as a blessing. He has something that no one can take from him. The day his grandmother was given her eternal life with her Savior!

Chapter 17

Honoring Your Loved One

Calls were made, and everyone had been notified. I had already pre-arranged Mom's memorial service, and it was paid for. That had been suggested by the Rowlett facility, so we could get her qualified for Medicaid.

Arranging a funeral for someone while they are very much alive is difficult. I prayed really hard before, during, and after I had everything picked out. I wanted to make sure it was something everyone would be pleased with.

I called and asked all of my siblings if they wanted to go with me to do this, but none of them did. I knew it was hard, so I understood. I didn't want to do it, so I couldn't expect them to want to do it either.

June 11, 2021, was the day of her service. I wrote some things in my journal, but I wasn't sure if I was supposed to read them at Mom's service or not.

I was awakened by a need for quiet prayer. I prayed and asked the Lord for confirmation. I knew what Mom's wishes were for the service, as far as the message went. While everyone she loved was in one room, she wanted the gospel preached. Her heart's desire was for everyone to go to heaven with her. But what I had written was for her children.

Honoring your parents' wishes is something I believed, in my heart, was critical. After all, it is the one commandment with a promise,

> *Honor your father and your mother, so that*
> *you may live long in the land the LORD your God is*
> *giving you.* (Exodus 20:12)

Well, when I arrived at the funeral home that morning, confirmation was given. The exact words I asked Him to have said to me, were spoken by the director when I got there. I had to sit down when she said them.

Like Gideon, I laid out the fleece, and confirmation was given. This wasn't the first time this had happened. It always left me in awe, and this time a little weak-kneed.

We all went in and were seated. Bubba was on my right, holding Able. Liz was on my left, holding Cameron. Ashtyn and Briley were with their parents on the front row after Bubba. When the time came, I stood up and walked to the podium, to read what was written, but I had to take a breath to calm my heart first.

After I was done, I sat down. I couldn't stop crying when the song, "A Mother's Love," began to play. I felt a hand on my shoulder and realized it was Klay. I just put my hand on his. He was so caring, and I appreciated him for that. Able stared at me as I wept. He then crawled onto my lap, wrapping his sweet little arms around me. He was so tight against me as I held him, I could feel his little heart beating and mine with it. I just silently thanked God for all my babies.

I could see Ashtyn and Briley looking around their parents at me. I knew if given a chance, they would be right where Able was. Able stayed there until I stopped crying and then, went back to Bubba. As soon as Able was out of my lap, Cameron climbed into my lap. Honestly, I had the best seat in the house!

When the service ended, Ashtyn darted over to me and leaped into my lap, hugging my neck. Briley immediately sat down beside me and said, "Are you okay?"

I just pulled her in, kissed her on the head, and quietly told her I was fine. And that was not a lie. How could I have not been good? So young were these kids and yet so caring. What could I have ever done to deserve such love? My soul was so overwhelmed by them.

They were my example of the *grace* God has given. By definition, Christians understand *grace* to be a spontaneous gift from God to people—*generous, free, and totally unexpected and undeserved*—that takes the form of divine favor, love, clemency.

How beautiful is the very word *grace*.

After the service, we all gathered at my oldest son's house, Dustin. He and Hope are always such a support. Our little church, and Mom's, brought food for the family, which was more than appreciated.

When Mom was moved from her house to assisted living, Tina gathered up all the costume jewelry Mom had bought at garage sales throughout the years and placed it in a big bag. Mom loved that stuff, and she always tried to get us to take some of it. So on this day, I took the big bag and dumped it on a table for everyone to get something to remember Mom by.

Momma would've been so tickled to see just how much people loved it. Some just wanted something because it was a part of Mom. I watched and thought how happy she would be to see them making such a fuss over it.

Tracey kept trying to get me to take something. She always worries about people being treated fairly. But I had what I wanted. That was ten days with my mom, and quiet times no one will ever know about. Nothing on that table had any more value than those moments! I even felt like *they* may have been cheated a little.

Honoring someone you love should not be a hard thing to do, but we tend to make it that way. We focus on all the pain it causes us and not all that was given to us, from God through them.

I have now lost both my parents and a brother. I can tell you that I had my dad for thirty years, my mother for fifty-five, and my brother for thirteen. Even though the time varied on each of them, all three taught me more than anyone could understand.

Losing my brother showed me that there is a redemptive quality in everyone. My dad was saved before my brother died. He back-slid because of the way the church we were attending treated him. However, it took losing my brother for the scales to be removed from his eyes. He was shown how precious life is, and how quickly those things that are unappreciated can be removed.

He saw things a little differently. Yes, he still did things that did not honor God, but don't we all? All I know is that he appreciated his children a little more and didn't want to lose another one. I was allowed to see him love us. That was something his older children by different marriages didn't get to experience.

So out of the death of a child, came a realization of who God is. That realization allowed him to feel the pain of being a parent that only my mother had experienced thus far.

It also produced a better, more forgiving father. One that we would turn to when our mother drifted into darkness. He did the best that he could at the end of his life to be a better dad. He tripped and stumbled through it, but at least, he didn't give up on us. God worked even back then, and I didn't even realize it.

When my dad died, it brought us all to a realization that we are responsible for our own choices. He sometimes overcompensated for not being there in the early years, and that made us weak. I watched as my younger brother grew up instantly. He bought a house with some of what was given to us. He is what I would consider extraordinarily successful today. Not by the world's standards but by finding his way to being more honorable and seeking God through prayer. It's something that a lot of people don't even know about him. He stumbled and tripped as well, but he is, at least, seeking God and finding his way.

During the time of Dad's service, he had a neighbor that was very kind to us. She began to take our kids to church with her, which in turn I started going, which in turn triggered my husband into attending.

That alone was nothing short of a miracle. Bubba had been bitterly hurt by events in his life that involved the brutal death of his father and how the pastor and church dealt with his family.

By the kindness shown by her, Bubba was saved, and it was an instantaneous transformation. One that has produced three men, led by his example, into adulthood.

So through my father's death, came yet four more salvations and a godly head of the family. All because someone was Christlike, and God used them to love on us!

We still consider those two neighbors some of our most cherished friends.

Now with my mother's death, brought a great renewal. One that is constantly at the forefront of my mind these days. She exercised so much humility, grace, and forgiveness that it has made me want to be more like her.

Also, looking back on how the pain of losing my brother took her into a very dark place for a while, I have a new appreciation of what can happen if we don't choose life. I also know how important it is to not carry a bitter root around with us. It tends to hold us down and take our ability to see the true changes in a person as they happen.

When my mother lost my older brother in 1980, she changed. Before, she would have never told me I didn't deserve Bubba.

I will never forget the day she said to me as a fourteen-year-old, "I am not living my life for you kids. You will just leave me or die."

I will always believe that Mom genuinely had a mental breakdown when she lost him. She chose to hang onto the rocky ledge and not grab the hand of God.

Her whole life, up to that point, revolved around her kids. But she was so busy trying to keep herself together, that she didn't even understand what was happening. She was distancing herself to not get hurt anymore. The pain was too much for her, and she needed to protect herself somehow from it happening again.

A chain of bad decisions followed. Jeff and I eventually went to live with my dad. Little did I know, Satan used that to confirm my mother's feelings of "you will leave me or die."

Just remembering that triggered the understanding of why my mother was the way she was about certain things after that.

I believe when she decided to come back to Texas, it was a much-needed reconciliation with her children and grandchildren. Once she had moved so far away, it was hard, financially, to get back.

As mere humans, we tend to only be able to see things from our perspective and not try to walk in another's shoes. I only knew how it hurt for Mom to say or do things that hurt me. I never stopped to think that she was hurting too.

It doesn't matter how fast or slow the "goodbye" comes or how young or old your loved one is. Not all goodbyes are from death.

Some are the ending of a relationship. Whatever it is, it hurts. It causes emotions that words cannot describe and pain that is deeper than all other types of pain. I don't know how someone can manage without the hope of knowing they will see their loved one again. That only comes from salvation through Jesus Christ. That is where my hope lies today.

I have seen some parents lose a child. They go through the mourning stage but allow God to lift them up. Not that they don't revisit the pain, but that they make a conscience effort to not set up camp there.

On the other hand, I have seen parents lose their children, not always to death, and they allow their life to become a train wreck. Good news is that even a train wreck can be used to the glory of God.

My mother returning back home to us allowed a reunion with her loved ones and her God. It was a sweeter time because she had experienced the bitterness of the pain for far too long.

God used her to pull the bitter root that resided in me that I didn't even know existed. Her grace and forgiveness not only pulled it out but filled the hole left by it with a fertile soil that I pray God uses to grow a deeper vine of love for others as He loved me.

I know that some will never understand how the death of a loved one can be used to glorify God or how it even should.

However, what greater honor is there than remembering all the good things you were given from that life? Hold onto the things that they did, that enriched your existence.

It might have been their strength, their ability to love unconditionally, their smile, or giggles. It could've been their ability to teach you through their mistakes. It could be a laundry list of beautiful things.

What a tribute that can be! Again, old or young, good or bad, it all still has a purpose. One we may not understand. We are called to walk by faith, not by sight.

What a great way to honor your loved one!

Chapter 18

Pulling Bitter Roots of Loss

There is one last story of loss and restoration I would like to tell you. It begins in June of 1985. At approximately 2:30 AM, a call to 911 is made, reporting a house fire on a small street in our town.

When the fire department arrived, they find the whole front half of a house engulfed in flames. After the fire was put out, the neighbors were interviewed to see if anyone had seen anything or if they knew of anyone at home during the time of the fire.

Each neighbor told a story of different coming and goings that night at this house. It was a residence that has had a lot of activity as of late.

Four nights prior to the fire, the police were called to a domestic disturbance. The man who lived there was trying to break down the front door. After speaking with all the persons of the house, the man stayed, and his wife, daughter, and nephew left to go stay at a relative's house to let the situation cool off.

The night of the fire would start several young men on a course of events that would forever change each of their lives.

The man that lived in this house was my husband's father. He lived there with his current wife, Bubba's stepmother, and her nephew. His dad was not reported missing for at least two months, after the fire had been set to his house.

Later, an investigation began as to know his whereabouts. My husband was actually accused of either hiding his father or killing him.

At the time, he was only seventeen and that had a devastating effect on his life. His father would remain missing for a total of six months.

During this time, Bubba tried to live a normal life, but people can just be cruel. He was at the local skating rink, where he hung out on the weekends. A grown woman, with a daughter the same age as my husband, came into the skating rink and confronted him about the truck his dad had been driving when he went missing. From the story that I was told, she got very loud and very ugly about the truck. It apparently belonged to her father, and it went missing at the same time his father did.

She was yelling, "What did you do with my daddy's truck? We know you did something with it! Where is it?"

Needless to say, that this would have been hard for anyone but must have been horrible for a son, that did not know where his father was, had been accused of atrocities that were heart-wrenching and was just trying to keep his head above water.

December of 1985, the police got a tip that resulted in the arrest of two young men. One of them agreed to a plea bargain in exchange for taking them to the body of Bubba's father.

During his father's funeral, the pastor made several statements that were not only embarrassing to Bubba but just totally humiliating. This only fanned the flames that Satan had ignited by his lies to Bubba's heart.

A good friend of Bubba's dad told me that what his eulogy said to those there was, "The boys who murdered his father had done the world a favor. And if you didn't want to end up in hell just like him, you would change your ways."

I do not know if that was spoken or not, but it was what was heard by those present there that day. Now, I understood the betrayal Bubba must have felt.

Now, fast forward to June 1986. I met my husband when he was eighteen years old, and he was as lost as I was. He drank quite a bit and seemed to be angry and a little bitter at times.

I was a single mother, recently divorced, and just trying to make as good of a life as I could for my young son. He was my everything. I did not even let my husband meet my son until we had been dating for over six months.

We dated for about three years and ended up getting married when my son was four years old. We went on to have two more sons. Our little family was growing, and we had a good life. There was only one thing that was missing, and I felt the pull more and more each day. I knew we needed to have our children in church, learning about Jesus.

When I would approach the topic with my husband, he would shut me down by saying, "You go right ahead but don't expect me to go with you. I told you that I was not ever going back, and I mean it."

I could never wrap my head around that. He was raised in church, and his grandmother was a very godly woman. I had admired her a great deal, and I knew he respected her.

Bubba had told me a little about his church experiences growing up, and while some of them weren't good, they just didn't seem that bad.

I decided to talk to his mother about it all, and she told me a long story about why Bubba was so incredibly bitter toward God and the church.

When his dad was murdered, not only did the police accuse him of being involved at one point, but they had paved the way for great judgment from persons within the church he had been raised in.

Not only from the church but his father's family as well. I noticed he did not talk about that side of the family very much. I never pushed the issue because that was a topic he was sensitive about. Bubba did, however, have a good relationship with his grandfather on that side of the family.

After my dad died, I started going to church with my kids. The church was having revival, and my kids begged their daddy until Bubba gave in and decided to go.

During the first night of him being there, I thought he will never come back. I could tell he was uncomfortable and fidgeted a lot. The pastor that did the revival was great. He was really hitting home with his preaching.

Much to my surprise, Bubba did go back the second night. Once again, I noticed him "white knuckling" the pew in front of us during the invitation time. I was starting to get a little irritated with him. I knew it would not help to confront him about it, but being the wife I am, I gave in and said something to him anyway.

I asked him what he was doing? Why didn't he just give into whatever was pulling at him? I told him I would rather him stay at home if all he was going to do was fight it. Was that the right thing to say? Probably not because it resulted in a heated discussion.

Eventually, the pastor of the little church went to speak with Bubba. I remember watching as they stood beside our truck and talked. Then, I saw Bubba lowered his head and began to sob.

Finally! He surrendered! They prayed together, and I did not ask many questions on the way home. I figured he would tell me what and when he wanted me to know.

The next night, Bubba was ready before any of us, and we all loaded up to go for the final night of revival. We sang praise songs and then, the visiting pastor did something he had not done the previous nights.

He stood up and asked if there was anyone who would like to give testimony on this final night.

I got the shock of a lifetime when Bubba stood up! He never spoke in public, and he had not said anything about giving testimony. My kids just looked at me with a confused look on their little faces.

He tried to steady himself as everyone in the room fell silent. I grabbed the back of his leg to show my support. He began to sob intensely. Still the room was silent. No one moved.

He began, "My father was murdered in 1985. I was accused of having something to do with it until they finally found the two guys who killed him. I have never forgiven them for not only killing my dad but for making me an outcast in the town I grew up in and the church I belonged to."

Still, no one was moving, and you could have heard a pin drop. I could see women and men alike wiping their eyes. It felt like the oxygen was being sucked out of the room to me. My boys had started crying because they had never seen their father cry. I just pulled them close to let them know it was okay.

Bubba continued, "During my dad's funeral, the preacher pretty much said my father was in hell. I have never forgiven him for that either. I have been mad at those boys, God, and the church for a long time!"

By now, his face was soaking wet, and he was trembling. But he continued with a strength and courage I have never seen in a man before. "But tonight, I stand before you and my God, and I forgive the two who killed my father! I forgive the preacher for my father's funeral, and I want to except the salvation of Christ. I do not want to live in anger anymore. I give it all up tonight!"

The whole room was filled with sobbing, both men and women alike. As Bubba sat down beside me, a woman that was seated three pews in front of us stood up. We knew her as Nanny Tot. She turned around to face Bubba. What she said will be forever burned into my heart. Her eyes were filled with tears, and she said, "Bubba, I am so glad to hear that you forgive the boys who killed your father. Because one of them was my grandson! I needed to know you forgive him. Thank you for that. I love you and your little family."

Bubba began to sob even harder, and everyone gasped as she spoke. Bubba and I both were amazed at how God had orchestrated this whole night. How this woman was in the same place as him, so she could hear him herself!

After she sat down, the visiting pastor stood and looked at Bubba. He began to speak with gentleness, "Bubba, the preacher who performed your father's funeral is my best friend. He has never forgiven himself for that day. He has spoken of it often and has worried about the damage he might have caused. I called him and let him know you forgave him tonight."

Again, the room was now visibly shaken by the intensity of the situation.

For three more hours, one man after another stood up and gave testimony and released bitter roots they held for someone. It was as if the Holy Spirit popped the top off that little church that night and filled it with Its presence. There was nothing being held back.

I had never been witness to anything like that before! My husband was changed that night! It was instantaneous, and he has not backslidden since. He is constant, and he is a praying, God-fearing, Spirit-filled, born again Christian. Not perfect but definitely redeemed and restored!

I wanted this story to be told, so you can know what choosing life in the middle of loss, pain, and anger can do. It is real! It is not earned, attained through being good, or even just forgiving. It is a gift! No one is too far gone that they cannot receive it just for the asking.

There is so much more to the story of my husband's experience. But the most important part is that he stepped out of the darkness and choose life!

Epilogue

There is a lot of pain, anxiety, fear, and loneliness in this world right now due to the COVID pandemic. Not only from the pandemic but due to this country turning its back on God.

I had found myself fearing what would happen if I or a loved one contracted COVID. I had seen enough death from it and knew it could have serious consequences.

Why was I living in fear? How was I going to shake this? After all, I lost my mother, and it was not even to COVID.

While writing this book, I did come down with COVID as did my husband, son, and daughter-in-law.

As He had so many times, God used His Word to speak directly to me. I had been doing a study in Ecclesiastes, and it was a very comforting book for me.

There is absolutely nothing under the sun that is not already known by God! No amount of worrying or fretting will change a thing. God is now and will always be in control, so why waste my time trying to change things that have already been written? I will not die the day before or the day after He has decided. In addition to that, life outside of God has no meaning. When we live in fear of diseases, our freedom being taken away or anything else for that matter, we are living outside of where God would have us to be.

In the old prophesies, like Jeremiah, God used Babylon to bring His people back to Him. If we stop to think what is going on all around us now, we have the chance to put our faith into action. Maybe this time is our Babylon as a country. We need to submit fully to God. We just accept and move toward the cross every day. Stop looking away at everything happening around us and look toward the cross.

Could this be a time that God is using to give us a chance at real restoration with Him? To learn humility again? I cannot be sure, but what I know is life with humility and trust in the great "I am" is a lot easier to live than a life without Him.

That is easy to say and harder to do; however, it is very doable. I do not live in a foreign land. I live right here with you.

We cannot live in constant fear or pain. Being held down by that is the most spiritually restrictive place you will ever be in.

Yes, this country is in a mess. Yes, this pandemic is real. Yes, we face each day with not being promised tomorrow.

I talk with people, on a daily basis, that struggle with this pandemic and the current leadership of this country. I have allowed their stress to become mine and listened as they are filled with anxiety on how to beat this thing.

It is a battle I fight every day and will continue to fight. I stop and ask myself daily, "Who is in control?"

Restoration comes from making a conscience effort to choose life. Relief from all the chaos comes from a relationship with the Lord. But again, it does require effort on our part.

Like having a surgery that will require rehabilitation. In order for us to return to some form of normalcy, we have to work at it.

There's an old saying, *"Nothing worth having comes easy."*

We will all face death one day. It's a given. What we choose to do with the time we have left is important. If we choose to live it in fear, then it is wasted. If we chose to live it to the fullest, it can be a time of great restoration.

My mother chose to step back into the light, praise God in heaven for that! In doing so, she was restored. Her final years were filled with the laughter, hugs, and kisses of her grandchildren and great-grandchildren.

Seasons come and go. Life continues after the loss. How can one continue while suffering such pain?

The only stability I have been allowed to have rests in the person of Jesus Christ. He is steady and reliable. Not once has He failed me the way I have failed Him, yet His love for me has not wavered.

If you have lost a loved one for whatever reason, I am sorry. I do not fully understand why things happen the way that they do. It's hard to see the good die young while the wicked can live long lives.

The thing we must remember is that we live in a fallen world that is tainted by sin, which has caused chaos and unpredictability. Our country is living proof of such a fallen world.

But here are a few things I have come to realize:

My brother died at an early age. He was on the cusp of manhood but never allowed to fully get there. He died in a way that was very tragic and hard for me to understand. He never got to see his son or granddaughters and how beautiful they are. He never got to experience the high of becoming a parent.

However, I remember what a gentle spirit he had and how he loved so intensely. I am glad that God didn't make him face the world we live in today or see what my family has had to endure. It would've been pure torture for him. That could be why He took him so early. I don't know. But I trust the one who does. It allows me to walk by faith, not by sight.

All I know is that facing all the pain, anxiety, and fear, and still being allowed to have joy and peace, is just not possible without Christ!

He takes all the hurt on. He begins to restore us. He *chose* to die so that I might live. We have the gift of eternal life because of how He chose to live and die for us.

> *I am the way, and the truth, and the life.*
> *No one comes to the Father except through me.*
> (John 14:16)

Jesus was only thirty-three years old when he was crucified. Thirty-three years well spent and a lot was gained in such a short time. A gift given and not deserved by the likes of me.

When Jesus left, he sent the Holy Spirit as the comforter. His word is full of life and stories that will give you the peace and rest you seek. So many people that God chose were only common people. They had the same flaws we suffer with today, but they were the ones he used to change the world.

Remembering that time is a gift is one way to come face-to-face with your mortality. How do you want to use it? Will your life be a gift to those around you or that you love?

Life is hard, and it will keep coming even after you accept the gift of salvation offered by Christ Jesus. But now, you have one that will never leave you, and you will face it together.

Find a Bible-based church. It is important to become a part of the body of Christ.

No, you cannot sit at home and have church all by yourself. Scripture is clear on that: *"Not neglecting to meet together, as is the habit of some, but encouraging one another, and all the more as you see the Day drawing near"* Hebrews 10:25.

If you are tired and filled with pain or anxious and fearful of the times we live in, stop allowing the torment. I urge you to hit your knees and seek Him. He is real, and He is there. I can speak from experience.

But even more to the point, don't take my word for it. I am not a Bible scholar, nor do I have a degree in theology. I am a common person living life just like you.

You have the responsibility to, not only yourself but to those you love, find out for yourself if you have not already.

And if you have already accepted the gift of salvation yet you are suffering, step back into the light. Seek harder, scream, and cry out! He already sees your heart, so you aren't hiding anything. Ask for prayer from those you trust. Stop your torment! Trust and reach for the hand of God, which will pull you up off that rocky ledge.

I have seen great things happen over the last few years. I have seen people step up and mend many fences. I have seen people come together for the greater good.

Turn off the TV and look around. God is all around us! There is still laughter and giving of ourselves. He is still very much alive and wanting us to see Him. Nothing we do is going to change tomorrow; however, we have the opportunity to enjoy today versus life in fear and pain.

May God bless you in ways you cannot even imagine! And remember, eyes on Him!

About the Author

Tonette Blasius has a passion for telling others about how great her God is. She is greatly inspired by those around her and considers herself a common woman, blessed beyond measure. Romans 8:28, "And we know that all things work together for good to those who love God," has been confirmed in her life repeatedly.

She has a second book coming out called *Bitter Roots*. It is based on a true story of how God used the brutal and tragic murder of a father to transform a bitter son into a godly and honorable man.

CPSIA information can be obtained
at www.ICGtesting.com
Printed in the USA
BVHW061124210322
632004BV00004B/171